WORLD BANK WORKING PAPE

# Higher Education Quality Assurance in Sub-Saharan Africa

## *Status, Challenges, Opportunities, and Promising Practices*

**Peter Materu**

Africa Region Human Development Department

THE WORLD BANK
Washington, D.C.

Manufactured in the United States of America
First Printing: August 2007

 printed on recycled paper



1 2 3 4 5 10 09 08 07

World Bank Working Papers are published to communicate the results of the Bank's work to the development community with the least possible delay. The manuscript of this paper therefore has not been prepared in accordance with the procedures appropriate to formally-edited texts. Some sources cited in this paper may be informal documents that are not readily available.

The findings, interpretations, and conclusions expressed herein are those of the author(s) and do not necessarily reflect the views of the International Bank for Reconstruction and Development/The World Bank and its affiliated organizations, or those of the Executive Directors of The World Bank or the governments they represent.

The World Bank does not guarantee the accuracy of the data included in this work. The boundaries, colors, denominations, and other information shown on any map in this work do not imply any judgment on the part of The World Bank of the legal status of any territory or the endorsement or acceptance of such boundaries.



ISBN-13: 978-0-8213-7272-2
eISBN: 978-0-8213-7273-9
ISSN: 1726-5878 DOI: 10.1596/978-0-8213-7272-2

Peter Materu is a Senior Education Specialist in the Africa Region Human Development Department of the World Bank.

**Library of Congress Cataloging-in-Publication Data**

Materu, Peter (Peter Nicolas)
Higher education quality assurance in Sub-Saharan Africa : status, challenges, opportunities and promising practices / Peter Materu.
p. cm. -- (Africa region human development)
ISBN 978-0-8213-7272-2
1. Education, Higher--Africa, Sub-Saharan. 2. Total quality management in higher education--Africa, Sub-Saharan. 3. Quality assurance--Africa, Sub-Saharan. I. Title.

LA1503.M345 2007
378.68--dc22

2007025148

# Contents

## List of Table



## List of Box

# Foreword

Concern about the quality of higher education is on the rise in Africa. It comes at a time of growing recognition of the potentially powerful role of tertiary education for growth, and it is a natural response to public perception that educational quality is being compromised in the effort to expand enrollment in recent years; growing complaints by employers that graduates are poorly prepared for the workplace; and increasing competition in the higher education market place as numerous private and transnational providers enter the scene. Little is available in the literature on what African countries are doing to regulate and improve higher education quality, what it takes to implement these initiatives, what has been the impact, and what are the priorities for capacity building.

This report maps and assesses the status and practice of higher education quality assurance (QA) in Sub-Saharan Africa. It centers on quality assurance in degree-granting tertiary institutions, but also incorporates, where available, information on other types of tertiary education. A main finding is that structured national-level quality assurance processes in African higher education are a very recent phenomenon and that most countries face major capacity constraints. Only about a third of them have established structured national quality assurance mechanisms, often only as recently as during the last ten years. Activities differ in their scope and rigor, ranging from simple licensing of institutions by the minister responsible for higher education, to comprehensive system-wide program accreditation and ranking of institutions. Within institutions of higher learning, self assessment and academic audits are gradually being adopted to supplement traditional quality assurance methods (for example, use of external examiners). However, knowledge about and experience with self-assessments is limited.

The main challenges to quality assurance systems in Africa are cost and human capacity requirements. Operating a national quality assurance agency typically entails an annual budget of at least US$450,000 and requires appropriately trained and experienced staff. In addition, the direct cost of accreditation averages an estimated US$5,200 per institution and US$3,700 per program. The costs of a full scale QA system are therefore unaffordable for most Sub-Saharan African countries. In countries with large tertiary systems, the report recommends institutional rather than program accreditation as a cost-effective option. In most other countries, where tertiary systems are small and underdeveloped, a less formal "self-assessment" for each institution may be necessary until the capacity could be strengthened to support a more formal national QA agency in the long run.

As African countries look to tertiary education to make a significant contribution to economic growth and competitiveness, improvements in the quality of programs and institutions will be critical. My hope is that the publication of this report will stimulate a lively debate about the nature of the issues and possible options for addressing them. If in the process the report encourages policymakers and their development partners to treat QA as a key component of strategies to improve higher education, it would have achieved its main objective of putting the spotlight on a long-neglected issue.

**Yaw Ansu**
Director
Human Development
Africa Region
The World Bank

# Acknowledgments

This report summarizes the findings from a study on quality assurance for higher education in Sub-Saharan Africa. The research was conducted between November 2005 and December 2006 through document and web reviews, interviews and six detailed country case studies covering Cameroon, Ghana, Mauritius, Nigeria, South Africa and Tanzania. The report was written by Peter Materu and incorporates materials produced by Fred Hayward (senior consultant) and the country case study researchers, namely Dan Ncayiyana (South Africa), Munzali Jibril (Nigeria), Paschal Mihyo (Tanzania) and Yaw Saffu (Ghana). Jane Njuru served ably as research assistant.

Within the World Bank, Halil Dundar, Michael Crawford, and Richard Hopper contributed as peer reviewers. Helpful comments were also received from William Saint, Jamil Salmi, Gary Theisen, Mourad Ezzine, and Xiaonan Ciao.

Various individuals involved in higher education within Africa provided useful inputs to the country case studies. Their contribution is highly acknowledged. The report was financed by the Norwegian Education Trust Fund and the World Bank.

# Acronyms and Abbreviations

| Acronym | Description | Countries where acronym is used |
|---|---|---|
| AAU | Association of African Universities | All African countries |
| APQN | Asia Pacific Region has established a Quality Assurance Network | Asia-Pacific Region |
| AQAA | Accreditation and Quality Assurance Agency | Madagascar |
| CAMES | *Conseil Africain et Malgache pour l'Enseignement Supérieur* | 16 Francophone countries |
| CHE | Commission for Higher Education | Kenya |
| CHESR | Council of Higher Education and Scientific Research | Cameroon |
| CHE | Council on Higher Education | South Africa |
| CNAQ | National Commission of Accreditation and Evaluation of Higher Education | Mozambique |
| CNE | *Comite National d'Evaluation* | Tunisia |
| DRC | Democratic Republic of Congo | DRC |
| ECZ | Examination Council of Zambia | Zambia |
| EVAC | Evaluation and Accreditation Corporation | Sudan |
| GATS | General Agreement on Trade in Services | All |
| HE | Higher Education | All |
| HEIs | Higher Education Institutions | All |
| HEAC | Higher Education Accreditation Council | Tanzania |
| HEQC | Higher Education Quality Committee | South Africa |
| HERQA | Higher Education Relevance and Quality Assurance Agency | Ethiopia |
| ICT | Information and Communication Technologies | All |
| IDA | International Development Agency | All |
| INQAAHE | International Network for Quality Assurance Agencies in Higher education | 55 countries |
| IUCEA | Inter-University Council of East Africa | Kenya, Tanzania, Uganda |
| LAC | Latin America & Caribbean | 30 countries |
| MBA | Masters in Business Administration | All countries |

| | | |
|---|---|---|
| NAB | The National Accreditation Board | Ghana |
| NBTE | National Board for Technical Education | Nigeria |
| NCHE | The National Council for Higher Education | Uganda, Namibia, Zimbabwe |
| NCPHE | National Commission on Private Higher Education | Cameroon |
| NEB | National Equivalence Board | Cameroon |
| NQF | National Qualifications Framework | Southern Africa |
| NUC | National Universities Commission | Nigeria |
| ODEL | Open and Distance e-learning | All |
| PRSP | Poverty Reduction Strategy Paper | All IDA countries |
| QA | Quality Assurance | All |
| QRAA | Quality Relevance and Assurance Agency | Ethiopia |
| SADC | Southern African Development Community | Southern Africa |
| SADCC | Southern African Development Coordination Conference | Southern Africa |
| SADCQF | SADC Qualifications Framework | Southern Africa |
| SAQA | South Africa Qualification Framework | South Africa |
| SARUA | Southern African Regional Universities Association | Southern Africa |
| TCCA | Technical Committee on Certification and Accreditation | Southern Africa |
| TEC | Tertiary Education Commission | Mauritius |
| UNISA | University of South Africa | South Africa |

# Executive Summary

Tertiary education is central to economic and political development, and vital to competitiveness in an increasingly globalizing knowledge society. In the case of Africa, tertiary education plays a critical capacity building and professional training role in support of all the Millennium Development Goals (MDGs). Recent research findings indicate that expanding tertiary education may promote faster technological catchup and improve a country's ability to maximize its economic output (Bloom, Canning, and Chan 2006). A new range of competences, such as adaptability, team work, communication skills, and the motivation for continual learning, have become critical. Thus, tertiary institutions are challenged to adjust their program structures, curricula, teaching and learning methods to adapt to these new demands. In recognition of this challenge, greater attention is being focused on quality assurance as a critical factor to ensuring educational relevance. The World Bank's *Constructing Knowledge Societies: New Challenges for Tertiary Education* underscores the importance of establishing robust quality assurance systems as necessary instruments for addressing today's challenges (World Bank 2002).

Sub-Saharan Africa (SSA), with about 740 million people, some 200 public universities, a fast increasing number of private higher education institutions and the lowest tertiary gross enrollment ratio in the world (about 5 percent), is now paying greater attention to issues of quality at the tertiary level. Rapid growth in enrollments amidst declining budgets during the 1980s and 1990s, the proliferation of private provision of higher education and pressure from a rapidly transforming labor market have combined to raise new concerns about quality. Countries are becoming conscious of the need for effective quality assurance and quality improvement. Senior officials from various countries, including Ethiopia,[1] Madagascar,[2] South Africa,[3] and Nigeria,[4] have expressed concern about the need to improve quality of tertiary institutions, the need to reassure the public about the quality of private providers, and the importance of ensuring that tertiary education offered in both public and private tertiary institutions meets acceptable local and international standards. Those concerns, together with the need to collect data on quality factors so that policy

1. On Ethiopia's efforts to improve quality, see: World Bank Sector Study, "Higher Education Development for Ethiopia: Pursuing the Vision," April 2004, pp. 57; 61–65.

2. The Minister of National Education for Madagascar, in a presentation at the World Bank on March 22, 2005 emphasized that the "Ministry should focus on quality control"—that focusing "more and more on quality" was to be part of their "new orientation."

3. Address by the Minister of Education, Professor Kader Asmal at the Southern African University Vice Chancellors Conference: *Engaging with the challenge in regional higher education to determine an effective leadership response.* Cape Town, South Africa, October 22, 2003.

4. Keynote address by Peter Okebukola, Executive Secretary, National Universities Commission, Nigeria at the Lagos State education summit, July 2006.

decisions regarding higher education can be based on evidence are echoed in other parts of the world.[5]

Several factors contributed to the decline in quality of higher education in Africa. These include a decline in per unit costs (from US$6,800 in 1980 to US$1,200 in 2002) amid rapidly rising enrollments; insufficient numbers of qualified academic staff in higher education institutions as the result of brain drain, retirements and HIV/AIDS; low internal and external efficiency; and poor governance. These factors, along with the rapid emergence of private providers in response to the increasing social demand for higher education, have prompted institutions and governments to put in place various forms of quality assurance mechanisms in an attempt to reverse the decline in quality and to regulate the new providers. Though some attempts to document these developments have been made by various individuals, no comprehensive mapping and analysis of quality assurance systems in the region has yet been undertaken.

This report communicates the results of the first steps to map and to assess higher education quality assurance (QA) in Sub-Saharan Africa. One purpose of the study is to establish a baseline on the status of quality assurance in higher education in Africa. A second is to provide information to education policymakers, stakeholders (including employers) and development partners involved in tertiary education in Africa that may assist them with identification and prioritization of capacity enhancement needs for quality improvement. For the purpose of this study, quality is defined as "fitness for purpose," that is, meeting or conforming to generally accepted standards as defined by an institution, quality assurance bodies and/or appropriate academic and professional communities. The study focused primarily on quality assurance in degree-granting tertiary institutions (here referred to as higher education institutions—HEIs). Yet, it also includes, where available, information on other types of tertiary institutions. An exhaustive treatment of all tertiary institutions was not done because wide differences in the types of these institutions exist between one country and the next, making comparison difficult. Information on quality assurance for this non-university tertiary group is also less readily available than that pertaining to degree-granting institutions.

This research was based on a desk and web study of published information on quality assurance in all 52 countries of Sub-Saharan Africa, supplemented by key informant interviews and six detailed country case studies (Cameroon, Ghana, Mauritius, Nigeria, South Africa and Tanzania). The case study countries were selected using the following criteria:

- Evidence that the case will illustrate major issues and serve as an example of good practice in quality assurance, quality improvement, and accreditation;
- Utility of the case to on-going and planned World Bank operations in the region;
- Existence of both public and private tertiary institutions in the country;

5. In September 2005 India's Prime Minister stated that India's universities were "falling behind their peers around the world" and spoke of the "need to make India's institutions of higher education and research world class." He argued that investments in higher education institutions and research and development are as important as investments in physical capital and physical infrastructure. See *Chronicle of Higher Education*, "India's Prime Minister Sharply Criticizes Universities as Lagging Behind." September 2, 2005. Pakistan's 5 Year Plan for higher education is recognition of the fact that "knowledge is now the engine for socioeconomic development" and an effort to create "the necessary foundations in which excellence can flourish and Pakistan can embark on the road to develop a knowledge economy." Prof. Atta-ur-Rahman, Higher Education Commission, *Medium Term Development Framework 2005–10*, p. iii.

- Experience with quality audits and/or accreditation;
- Willingness of the respective institutions and/or national body to participate in the study; and
- Evidence of effective quality assurance and improvement activities at the institutional and/or national level.

## Key Findings and Conclusions

### *Status of Quality Assurance at the National Level*

Quality of higher education and the need for effective quality assurance mechanisms beyond those of institutions themselves are becoming priority themes in national strategies for higher education. This is driven by the importance attached to higher education as a driver of growth and in achieving the MDGs, on one hand, and the emergence of new types of higher education providers (beyond public institutions), on the other. At the institutional level, increasing demand for accountability by governments, other funders and the public, coupled with the desire to be comparable with the best in-country and internationally is pushing HEIs to pay more attention to their QA systems.

Structured QA processes in higher education at the national level are a very recent phenomenon in most African countries but the situation is changing rapidly. Existing QA agencies are young, the majority having been established within the last 10 years. Currently 16 countries have functioning national QA agencies. The emergence of private tertiary institutions and the need to regulate their activities appears to have been the main trigger for the establishment of formal QA agencies in most countries. Perhaps because of this historical fact, the main purpose of QA agencies in Africa has been regulation of the development of the sector rather than to enhance accountability and quality improvement. Several countries have now changed their laws to make accreditation of public institutions mandatory. As of now, national agencies of Ethiopia Ghana, Mauritius, Nigeria, South Africa, Tanzania, and Uganda are directed to oversee quality assurance in both public and private institutions. Tanzania and Uganda amended their laws within the last two years to extend the mandate to public universities while Ethiopia's mandate included all types of HEIs right from its inception in 2003. Mozambique and Madagascar are developing their systems aiming at a similar approach. This positive step needs to be buttressed by an effective incentive system (currently absent) in order to encourage compliance and hence, quality improvement. Also needed is a stronger link between the results of QA processes and funding allocations, as well as learning outcomes (quality of graduates), in order to promote accountability.

There is convergence in methodology across countries. At the national level, three different types of quality assurance practices can be observed: institutional audits, institutional accreditation, and program accreditation. But irrespective of the approach taken, a convergence among these methodologies is becoming apparent. Evidence from country case studies shows that all QA agencies follow the same basic approach—which is similar to that followed by QA agencies in developed countries. This approach entails an institutional (or program) self-assessment, followed by a peer review and transmission of findings to the institution, the government and even to stakeholders. This tends to be the norm regardless of whether it is an audit or accreditation. When conducted properly, this is a rigorous process which produces useful data that can be used for strategic planning and other purposes. However, experience from the case study countries shows that the methodology demands a high level of human and financial capacity. In a situation where the pool of qualified human resources is already strained, not all countries can afford to set up a full scale national agency. In fact, it is not justifiable for countries with small tertiary education systems.

The process is as important as the outcome. Experience from institutions within case study countries shows that the self-assessment process (at institutional or unit level) has positive effects on the culture of quality within an institution or unit. Because it is conducted within a collegial atmosphere without any pressure from an external body, the self-assessment fosters social cohesion and teamwork among staff and also enhances staff accountability of the results of the process. More concretely, self-assessment also helps institutions to identify their own strengths and weaknesses, while generating awareness of key performance indicators. The process of self-assessment is widely seen as the most valuable aspect of quality assurance reviews because it helps institutions to build capacity from within. This capacity-building function of self-assessment is valuable in any context, but it is particularly important in the countries of Sub-Saharan Africa where capacity remains very weak. Self-assessment is also less costly than accreditation and can be conveniently planned within an institution's annual calendar. Thus, irrespective of whether a country has a full-scale national QA agency or not, regular self-assessments at the institutional and unit levels are the backbone of a viable quality assurance system.

The standards being applied by national QA agencies are mainly input-based with little attention being paid to process, outputs and outcomes. However, in almost all countries, no link between quality assurance results and funding allocations can be found. The most common QA standards in the case studies are mission and vision, academic programs, library resources, physical and technological resources, number and qualifications of staff, number of students and their entry qualifications, and financial resources (relative to number of students). The study found no evidence of output standards such as through-put ratio (percent of a cohort that graduates within a specified time) or volume and quality of research. There was also no evidence of any link between quality assurance results and funding allocations to institutions or units.

Francophone Africa lags behind the rest of Africa in developing structured management of quality assurance at the national level and also within institutions of higher learning. Only Mauritius and Cameroon have national QA agencies. Madagascar is currently in the process of setting up one. CAMES, which has hitherto been responsible for quality assurance in the entire francophone region, presently appears over-stretched in capacity. Moreover, it lacks the mandate to enforce quality standards as participation in its activities is voluntary. But increasing concern about the need to pay more attention to higher education quality at the country level is emerging within francophone Africa. Many institutions are using their on-going reforms of shifting to the LMD system as an opportunity to address quality issues. Based on the findings of this study, countries with very small tertiary education systems (for example, Niger, Chad, Mali, etc.) would be best advised to adopt a sequential development approach that begins with institutional self-assessments.

Professional associations are actively involved in Quality Assurance. However, in some countries, their mandates overlap with those of existing national QA agencies. Unlike national agencies, professional associations fund their activities from membership fees. In some countries, these associations are deeply involved in the accreditation process. In all the case study countries, professional associations are represented in accreditation panels, in addition to their regular role in certifying/licensing graduates to practice as professionals. With the exception of South Africa, the standards applied by professional bodies are not harmonized with those applied by national QA agencies. In Nigeria, discussions towards harmonization of quality standards are underway. Because of the overlapping mandates, the potential contribution of these associations to national QA efforts is yet to be fully tapped.

Although in some cases the establishing laws describe QA agencies as independent bodies, in reality all existing QA agencies are highly dependent on government. They rely almost entirely on public funding and their governing bodies and top management are appointed by government. However, some (for example, Egypt, Nigeria and South Africa) enjoy significant autonomy in their operations. The fact that both the agencies and the public institutions under their jurisdiction depend on government funding raises questions as to the legitimacy of requests by these agencies that institutions comply with quality improvement requirements unless this is accompanied by adequate government funding to address the problems identified.

The activities of existing national QA systems differ in their scope and rigor, varying from simple licensing of institutions by the minister responsible for higher education (for example, DRC) to comprehensive, system-wide program accreditation and ranking of institutions (for example, Nigeria); and from tight government control to semi-autonomous QA processes. Only CAMES, Mauritius, Nigeria and South Africa conduct program accreditation. The rest carry out institutional accreditation. This is the most common practice and has been limited to private institutions; no public institution has been subjected to a full institutional accreditation process. Nigeria has started preparations to that end with a planned launch date of 2007. The level of independence and professionalism within QA agencies also differs widely. The Higher Education Quality Committee in South Africa, for example, directly defends its budget in parliament whereas in Cameroon, the agency is funded as a department of the Ministry for Higher Education and the minister has the final say in accreditation decisions. This heterogeneity in activity and rigor raises doubts as to the ability of some tertiary education systems to respond to global challenges such as the Bologna Process, which is intended to harmonize tertiary systems in the European Union area, leading to a common framework for recognition of programs, credentials and competencies.

## *Quality Assurance within Higher Education Institutions*

Within institutions of higher learning, use of external examiners, self-evaluation and academic audits are the most common forms of quality assurance processes. Institutions readily accept self-assessment because it empowers them and their staff to take charge of the quality of their performance without the pressure usually associated with an external review. Self-assessment also helps institutions to identify their own strengths and weaknesses, while generating awareness of key performance indicators. As noted above, it is the process of self-assessment that is widely seen as the most valuable aspect of quality assurance processes. The capacity-building function of self-assessment is particularly important in the countries of Sub-Saharan Africa where capacity remains very weak. In a few institutions (for example, the University of Dar es Salaam in Tanzania), these processes existed even before the establishment of national QA agencies. At present, self-evaluation is increasingly being done as preparation for accreditation (for example, in Nigeria, South Africa and Tanzania). However, expertise in conducting self evaluation/academic audits is limited within Africa. Strengthening professional capacity in these areas is a major recommendation of this study.

Public HEIs are the key resource base for Quality Assurance Systems. Countries with national QA agencies rely heavily on higher education institutions for their professional staff, peer review panels and governance. By nature, quality assurance methods require academic peers to staff their appraisal teams. This can weigh heavily on countries where only a small number of qualified individuals are available to perform the tasks necessary. Given the limited number of senior academic staff in African HEIs, complaints arise that participation by senior staff in national QA processes is causing considerable work overload as these responsibilities are normally carried out above and beyond their normal duties. The shortage of qualified personnel is one of the major constraints to developing widespread and effective quality assurance practices in the region.

Although it is too early to draw a general conclusion, evidence from Nigeria suggests that accreditation is increasing accountability among public and private institutions of higher learning. As a consequence, institutional leaders are paying greater attention to quality improvement.

### *Regional Collaboration in Quality Assurance*

The need for regional collaboration in higher education is progressively being recognized, but difficulties exist in turning this recognition into effective mechanisms for mutual assistance. Regional QA networks are particularly relevant to Africa because of the human resource constraints. They can support the emergence QA practices where none exist, and can provide assistance to small and/or struggling national QA systems. Several subregional QA initiatives are currently under discussion. At the continental level, the Association of African Universities (with support from the World Bank and other development partners) plans to launch a QA capacity-building program in 2007, possibly leading to a regional network on quality assurance. Despite recognition of the value of regional collaboration, especially to small countries, existing regional initiatives have yet to be effective. Without national governments to fund them and a legal instrument to enforce their mandates, these networks are highly dependent on the transient priorities of donor funding. Their activities focus largely on knowledge-sharing and capacity-building. At best, regional collaboration strives for voluntary accreditation, as is the case with CAMES.

### *Challenges and Capacity Enhancement Needs*

Technical capacity is the most pressing constraint in national QA agencies. This manifests itself in three ways: (i) insufficient numbers of adequately trained and credible professional staff at the agencies to manage QA processes with integrity and consistency across institutions/programs and over time; (ii) inadequate numbers of academic staff in HEIs with knowledge and experience in conducting self-evaluations and peer review, especially in countries that conduct system-wide reviews (for example, South Africa and Nigeria); and (iii) strain on senior academic staff in HEIs as they have to support both their own internal quality systems as well as external quality assurance processes of their national agencies. This problem exists across the board, even in economically more advanced countries like South Africa.

QA costs money and time of highly-skilled individuals. Though effective, system-wide program accreditation is costly and involves large numbers of people and complex logistics. The cost per program accredited can be as high as US$5,000. For countries with many programs these costs could be unbearable if the exercise is to be done with quality. Added to this are the costs for running a national agency (estimated to be up to US$2 million per year) and costs to institutions for implementing improvements on programs that are found to be of inadequate quality. Without adequate funding, the quality of QA processes—and hence the credibility and integrity of their outcomes—are threatened. Countries need to make frank assessments of their financial capacity to undertake the range of possible QA activities and tailor their systems to their unique financial situations, as well as to their human resource constraints.

As in other regions, assuring the quality of distance learning and new modes of delivery remain a challenge. Although all the agencies reviewed have responsibility over distance and e-learning, none has yet conducted accreditation in these areas. In most cases, national standards do not exist or are under development. Considerations for ICT-facilitated cross-border provision of higher education have not been adequately factored into existing quality assurance systems. Development of quality standards and verification of compliance for distance education require new skills which are currently lacking in most countries. Capacity-building in this regard is urgent, considering the implications of the General Agreement on Trade in Services (GATS). Given that resources are limited, networking and experience sharing at subregional and regional levels would accelerate the rate of diffusion of these skills.

Little is known about the impact of quality assurance on the quality of graduates, employer attitudes towards graduates, and research outputs of tertiary institutions; that is, whether implementation of a rigorous QA system actually improves the quality of graduates that join the labor market and the research output of institutions. Though no studies have been undertaken, there are signs that employers are paying attention to the results of program accreditation and ranking of institutions. However, hardly any information can be found on the impact of these processes on the quality of graduates joining the labor market as well as on research output. Follow-up work on this subject is necessary as it would strengthen the case for increased investment in quality improvement.

## Options for Capacity Enhancement

To address the above challenges, the following options are suggested for consideration by policymakers, QA practitioners and development partners. Fuller discussion is provided in Chapter 7.

- *Adopt a stepwise development strategy*. Given existing pressure on HE systems and institutions to conform to international norms, a stepwise strategy is the most prudent approach. For most African countries, the emerging convergence on rigorous QA practices is unaffordable, given existing constraints in capacity. Each country needs to assess its capacity and structure its QA system to match available resources.

A general practice that has worked well elsewhere is to start gradually, taking time to pilot processes before full scale roll-out.

- *The responsibility for quality of higher education ultimately rests with the HEIs.* Capacity building efforts should be directed to building a culture of quality within HEIs. Without a strong culture of quality in institutions of higher learning, there is little chance of success at the national level.
- *Even in the absence of external accreditation, institutional academic reviews (academic audits) are an effective way to introduce a culture of quality into an institution.* A necessary pre-requisite is training of staff in self-evaluation and peer-reviewing. Involvement of peer reviewers from other institutions within or outside the country in self-assessment exercises can enrich the process, but selection must be done carefully to justify the high costs involved. Experience from the case studies shows that establishment of a dedicated quality assurance unit within an institution helps to ensure monitoring and evaluation of QA processes, maintains institutional memory and ensures implementation of recommended quality improvement measures.
- *For countries with large tertiary education systems and adequate capacity, institutional accreditation (rather than a system-wide program accreditation) is a more cost-effective way to get started with a national QA system.* It costs less, and the stress on HEIs and national QA agencies is less severe. Where cost is a main constraint, program accreditation should best be limited to professional programs and conducted in collaboration with professional associations.
- *Partnership with foreign institutions and QA agencies* with sound QA experience can help to supplement local capacity in the short-term and also bring in relevant experience from other regions. However, this must be weighed against the costs involved.
- *The need for technical assistance to develop quality standards is urgent, particularly as regards regulation of e-learning and cross border delivery of tertiary education.* Because expertise in this area is very limited in Africa, external assistance may be required.
- *Regional collaboration in quality assurance is particularly relevant to Africa,* given the large number of small countries with fragile economies and weak higher education systems. Desirable forms of regional collaboration include peer reviewing for accreditation purposes, regional accreditation agency instead of national ones (especially for small countries), common standards and guidelines for cross-border education, mechanisms for credit transfer and recognition of qualifications, and sharing of experiences. But for regional collaboration to work well, increased commitment by governments and continued assistance from international development partners are critically necessary.
- *Governments and national agencies are advised to consider reviewing tertiary education funding policies such that allocation of public resources to tertiary institutions is linked to quality factors as a strategy for encouraging institutions to undertake quality improvements.* Without such a linkage, effective response to quality assessment recommendations by public HEIs will be limited, and eventually, QA systems might lose credibility.
- *Further work on the link between QA and labor market needs is recommended.* This should ultimately be undertaken at the country level since size, mix and level of development differs widely from country to country.

## Possible Role of Development Partners

The World Bank and other development partners could play a catalytic role by using their education projects in African countries to provide technical assistance for training in institutions and in national QA agencies, development of quality standards for open and distance learning, institutional audits, and understanding of transnational higher education. Knowledge-sharing on QA experiences among Africa countries and with other regions in the world is particularly needed. Support could also take the form of seed funds for establishing quality improvement funds, and funding for regional and subregional higher education bodies (for example, the AAU, CAMES, SARUA and IUCEA) to strengthen their capacity to assist countries in their quality assurance activities, especially as regards quality assurance in small countries.

Long-term commitments of donor support are needed to provide implementation stability to regional initiatives. Despite high potential benefits, regional and subregional QA initiatives are the most vulnerable since they have to compete for budget resources with individual nations' priorities. Multilateral membership institutions like the World Bank and the African Development Bank are best suited to support regional initiatives because of their ability to convene and engage in dialogue with member countries, either individually or as a group. While short-term support remains useful as seed funds to get started, long-term commitment will be essential to provide stability during an interim period and enable QA initiatives to create a visible impact on the ground—a necessary condition for developing sustainable funding mechanisms.

CHAPTER 1

# Introduction

The notion of quality is hard to define precisely, especially in the context of tertiary education where institutions have broad autonomy to decide on their own visions and missions. Any statement about quality implies a certain relative measure against a common standard; in tertiary education, such a common standard does not exist. Various concepts have evolved to suit different contexts ranging from quality as a measure for excellence to quality as perfection, quality as value for money, quality as customer satisfaction, quality as fitness for purpose, and quality as transformation (in a learner) (SAUVCA 2002). Some institutions have adopted the International Standards Office (ISO) approach in some of their activities. Depending on the definition selected, quality implies a relative measure of inputs, processes, outputs or learning outcomes. Institutions, funders, and the public need some method for obtaining assurance that the institution is keeping its promises to its stakeholders. This is the primary goal of quality assurance.

This report describes and assesses higher education quality assurance in Africa at the program, institutional, and national levels. It also includes a brief commentary about regional efforts. It presents an overview of the status of quality assurance in higher education in Africa, discusses the challenges and opportunities for capacity enhancement and identifies examples of promising practices that could be emulated. The report summarizes the findings of a study conducted by the World Bank and is primarily intended to assist World Bank staff, partner organizations, and country counterparts in raising awareness concerning the importance of quality higher education and in identifying priority capacity-building needs. Given the large number of countries in Africa, it has not been possible to delve into the specifics of each country in detail. Thus, the conclusions and recommendations given here are only intended to act as a guide and would have to be adapted to the specific situation of each country.

A two-phase approach was adopted for the study. The first phase comprised a mapping exercise designed to obtain an overview of the status, scope and activity level of quality assurance in all the 52 countries of the continent. As expected, the amount of data available is limited. In most cases information is out of date since no comprehensive study on quality assurance in higher education in Africa had been conducted prior to this effort. Data collection relied on available published materials, websites of ministries of education and quality assurance agencies, other web-based sources, and interviews with officers responsible for quality assurance in the case study countries. The second phase comprised a detailed study of quality assurance processes in six country case studies (Cameroon, Ghana, Mauritius, Nigeria, South Africa, and Tanzania). These were selected on the basis of the following criteria:

- Evidence that the case will illustrate major issues and serve as an example of good practice in quality assurance, quality improvement, and accreditation;
- Utility of the case to on-going and planned World Bank operations in the region;
- Existence of both public and private tertiary institutions in the country;
- Experience with quality audits and/or accreditation;
- Willingness of the respective institutions and/or national body to participate in the study; and
- Evidence of effective quality assurance and improvement at the institutional and/or national level.

The purpose of the study was to establish a baseline on the status of quality assurance in higher education in Africa and to provide information and analysis to education policymakers, implementers and development partners involved in tertiary education in Africa—information and analysis needed to identify and prioritize capacity-building needs for quality improvement.

The study focused primarily on quality assurance in degree-granting higher education institutions. However, it includes, where available, information on other types of tertiary institutions. An exhaustive treatment of all tertiary institutions was not done because wide differences in the type of these institutions can be found between one country and other, making comparison difficult. Quality assurance information at the non-university level is also less readily available than for degree-granting institutions. The report also includes a discussion of QA initiatives at the subregional and regional levels as well as comments on the role played by professional bodies in ensuring quality of tertiary education.

## Definitions

Terms used in quality assurance are employed in a variety of ways and have different meanings in different parts of the world. For example, in the United States the term "accreditation" refers to a process of review and assessment of quality that result in a decision about whether or not to certify the academic standard of an institution. In the United Kingdom "accreditation" refers to a *Code of Practice* by which an institution without its own degree-awarding powers is given authority by a university or other awarding institution to offer its degrees to students meeting the requirements. In order to avoid ambiguity, the key terms[6] used in this study are defined in this section. Other related terms are defined in the appendixes.

- *Quality,* in the context of this report, refers to "fitness for purpose" meeting or conforming to generally accepted standards as defined by an institution, quality assurance bodies and appropriate academic and professional communities. In the diverse arena of higher education, fitness for purpose varies tremendously by field and program. A broad range of factors affect quality in tertiary institutions including their vision and goals, the talent and expertise of the teaching staff, admission and assessment standards, the teaching and learning environment, the employability of its graduates (relevance to the labor market), the quality of the library and laboratories, management effectiveness, governance and leadership.
- *Quality assurance* is a planned and systematic review process of an institution or program to determine whether or not acceptable standards of education, scholarship, and infrastructure are being met, maintained and enhanced. A tertiary institution is only as good as the quality of its teaching staff—they are the heart of the institution who produce its graduates, its research products, and its service to the institution, community, and nation.
- *Accreditation* is a process of self-study and external quality review used in higher education to scrutinize an institution and/or its programs for quality standards and need for quality improvement. The process is designed to determine whether or not an institution has met or exceeded the published standards (set by an external body such as a government, national quality assurance agency, or a professional association) for accreditation and is achieving its mission and stated purpose. The process usually includes a self-evaluation, peer reviews and site visits. Success results in accreditation of a program or an institution.
- *Audit* is a process of review of an institution or program to determine if its curriculum, staff, and infrastructure meet its stated aims and objectives. It is an evaluation of an institution or its programs in relation to its own mission, goals, and stated standards. The assessors are looking primarily at the success of the institution in achieving its own goals. An audit focuses on accountability of institutions and programs and usually involves a self-study, peer review and a site visit. Such an evaluation can be self-managed or conducted by external body. The key differences between an audit and accreditation is that that the latter focuses on standards external to the institution, usually national, and an assessment of the institution in terms of those standards. Audits focus on an institution's own standards and goals and its success in attaining them.
- An *academic review* is a diagnostic self-assessment and evaluation of teaching, learning, research, service, and outcomes based on a detailed examination of the curricula, structure, and effectiveness of a program as well as the quality and activities of its faculty. It is designed to give an institution an evaluation of its own academic programs based on a self-assessment by the unit, a peer review by colleagues outside

6. This glossary is modified and drawn from a lengthier version prepared by Fred M. Hayward for the Council for Higher Education Accreditation (CHEA) in February 2001. See: www.chea.org/international/inter_glossary01.html.

the program, and a report on the findings. Unlike an audit, an academic review can be limited to a single program and does not involve a site visit by reviewers external to an institution. In this report, the term "self assessment" is synonymous to "academic review."

- *Licensing* is a process for granting a new institution or program permission to launch its activities. It is sometimes a phased process whereby an institution goes through various stages before been granted a full license. In Tanzania, for example, applications to set up new institutions go through four licensing stages, each with specific requirements: letter of interim authority; certificate of provisional registration; certificate of full registration; and finally, certificate of accreditation.
- *Higher education institutions* (HEIs) are tertiary institutions whose legal mandates allow them to award degrees. These include universities and other forms of tertiary institutions, for example, the Ghana Institute of Public Administration (GIMPA).

The study team observed that in several African countries the term *accreditation* is used to refer to public universities that were established by acts of Parliament, by statute, or by decree. They are "accredited" *de jure* (by law) but not as the result of peer review, a site visit, and a report assessing the institution. Similarly, it was noted that the term *audit*, like accreditation, is also used in ambiguous ways to describe a variety of assessments of certain aspects of an institution rather than the whole institution. For the purpose of this study, an institution is considered to be accredited or audited if it has undergone the following processes:

- A self-study prepared by the institution or program.
- An external peer review process, including a site visit. Assessment is based on standards or criteria for the process set by the quality assurance agency or in the case of an audit, by the institution itself.
- A written report on the site visit which focuses on institutional academic quality standards, quality assurance processes, and recommended improvements.
- For accreditation (but not audits), a decision by an empowered national agency resulting from the review to accredit or deny accreditation, or assign some intermediate status such as *candidacy for accreditation* or *probation*.

This is essentially the model for quality assurance towards which the international community (including the African case study countries) appears to be converging. As discussed later in this report, completing all the tasks requires considerable capacity, which simply does not exist in many African countries. Alternative options for consideration are discussed in subsequent sections.

The main conclusions of this report could form the basis for capacity enhancement interventions and/or provide guidance to policymakers and higher education stakeholders in setting up quality assurance systems. The report is divided into seven chapters with suggestions for possible next steps in the final chapter. The topics of succeeding chapters are noted below:

- Chapter 2 builds the case for quality higher education as a building block for economic and social development in Africa. Starting with a review of the history of quality assurance in Africa, it explains why it is necessary and urgent for Africa to pay more attention to quality assurance at this point in time.

- Chapter 3 presents an analytical overview of the status of quality assurance systems at the institutional and national level, and also discusses the role of professional associations in quality assurance. The chapter includes a brief assessment of ongoing efforts to foster regional collaboration in higher education quality assurance in Africa, including lessons from these initiatives.
- Chapter 4 explores the cost implications of implementing quality assurance systems and identifies the key cost drivers.
- Chapter 5 analyzes the challenges confronting quality assurance systems in the continent and highlights opportunities for reform.
- Chapter 6 seeks to distill some of what could be termed *promising practices;* that is, practices that successfully address some of the challenges cited in previous chapters and/or appear worth emulating.
- Chapter 7 summarizes the main conclusions and options recommended for consideration by institutions, governments, the World Bank and other development partners in their efforts to improve of higher education in Africa.

# CHAPTER 2

# The Case for Quality Higher Education

## Why Quality Higher Education is So Important in Africa

Increasing importance of tertiary education to competitiveness and economic development. Changes brought about by the transition to a knowledge economy have created a demand for higher skill levels in most occupations. A new range of competences such as adaptability, team work, communication skills and the motivation for continual learning have become critical. Thus, countries wishing to move towards the knowledge economy are challenged to undertake reforms to raise the quality of education and training through changes in content and pedagogy. Recent studies have demonstrated that for developing countries, higher education can play a key "catch-up" role in accelerating the rate of growth towards a county's productivity potential (Bloom, Canning, and Chan 2006). The international community is also paying increased attention to this new thinking. The World Bank's Africa Action Plan (2005) underscores the critical importance of post-primary education in building skills for growth and competitiveness in low- and medium-income countries. The Plan includes among its core actions during 2007–09, the monitoring and assessment of the quality of post-primary education and training, and the development and implementation of operational plans for IDA support to technical, tertiary and research institutions in at least eight African countries by FY08 (World Bank 2005).

Higher Education is critical to achieving the EFA and Millennium Development Goals (MDGs). Higher Education institutions educate people in a wide range of disciplines which are key to effective implementation of MDGs. These include the core areas of health, agriculture, science and technology, engineering, social sciences and research. In addition, through research and advisory services, they contribute to shaping national and international policies. For example, with respect to the Education For All (EFA) Goal, although as far back as 1993, the League of World Universities concluded in its Rectors' Conference that

**Box 1: Acknowledging the HE Quality Problem in Africa—An Ethiopian Example**

"One of the major problems of African education is not as most think–universality; rather it is quality which is the problem. Africa needs thinkers, scientists, researchers, real educators who can potentially contribute to societal development. Most donors define African education success in terms of how many students are being graduated and how many students are in school. The quantity issue is of course one thing that should be addressed, but it shouldn't be the whole mark of any education intervention in Africa. How an African resource could be better utilized by an African child for an African development should be the issue."

Demeke Yeneayhu, Student, Addis Ababa University, Ethiopia, 2006

"universities cannot sit on the sidelines during the education crisis," links between higher education institutions and EFA in Africa have not been strong. This raises the question of whether the training provided by higher education institutions is consistent with new thinking advocated by EFA and, in general, with the new and emerging demands of the global agenda. An increased focus on quality and relevance of higher education would contribute to strengthening the link between higher education and various MDGs and more generally with the needs of the labor market.

Supporting other levels of education and buttressing other skill levels. Higher education plays a key role in supporting other levels of education (Hanushek and Wossmann 2007). This ranges from the production of teachers for secondary schools and other tertiary education institutions, to the training of managers of education and conducting research aimed at improving the performance of the sector. According to a recent study, low quality or lack of a critical mass of graduates at the secondary school level reduces the productivity of tertiary-educated workers and dampens the overall incentives for education investments (Ramcharan 2004). The study also shows that the presence of tertiary-educated workers in the workplace raises the productivity of medium-skills workers.

Increasing the value of investments to expand access. The challenge for Africa in creating knowledge economies is to improve the quality of tertiary education and at the same time increase the number of people trained at high quality levels in appropriate fields. The record to date in this area is not particularly good. Examples abound of rapid growth in the number of students in higher education while at the same time higher education quality drops substantially. As Box 1 illustrates, even the beneficiaries of tertiary education are beginning to demand quality.

## Why HE Quality Assurance Systems Are Needed

Every nation and its tertiary education graduates are competing in an environment shaped by their own local and national needs as well as international expectations and standards. With globalization, the impacts of international standards are increasing and public demand for transparency and accountability is on the rise. Educators and policymakers are therefore challenged to set appropriate standards of their own which draw on and reflect the unique history, needs, and expectations of their stakeholders. Furthermore, they are expected to put in place mechanisms to enforce those standards and to monitor performance of their tertiary education systems with a view to taking appropriate and timely measures to adapt to new realities. The main factors that drive the current push to strengthen quality assurance in higher education in Africa are discussed in the following paragraphs.

### *Increased Demand for Tertiary Education and Rising Private Contributions*

Since the late 1980s, the global market for tertiary education has been growing at an average rate of 7 percent per annum. Worldwide, more than 80 million tertiary students pursue their studies with the help of 3.5 million additional people who are employed in teaching and related work. Annual income from tuition fees is estimated to be over US$30 billion, increasingly from private sources. In South Korea, for example, 75 percent of tertiary education is privately funded. In Australia, tuition fees contribute more than US$4 billion annually to GDP, surpassing the earnings of the country's main agricultural products (wool and wheat). The USA presently hosts about 586,000 international students, most of whom pay tuition and fees. Global annual spending on tertiary education amounts to about US$300 billion or 1 percent of global economic output (Materu 2006). Without a robust system to ensure that programs offered are relevant to the socioeconomic needs of the society they serve, a HE system lacks a mechanism to promote and monitor the accountability of HE institutions to their stakeholders (students, parents, governments, and other funders).

### *Rapid Growth of Tertiary Enrollment in Africa Without a Matching Increase in Funding*

This global trend is reflected on the African continent. Between 1985 and 2002 the number of tertiary students increased by 3.6 times (from 800 thousand to about 3 million), on average by about 15 percent yearly. This trend was led by Rwanda (55 percent), Namibia (46 percent), Uganda (37 percent), Tanzania (32 percent), Cote d'Ivoire (28 percent), Kenya (27 percent), Chad (27 percent), Botswana (22 percent), and Cameroon (22 percent) (Materu 2006). Because public investment has not been able to keep up with this frantic pace, private investment in tertiary education is also on the rise in Africa. Out of roughly 300 universities operating today in Sub-Saharan Africa, about one-third are privately funded. The majority of these have been established since the year 2000. Private participation in tertiary education has undoubtedly made a significant contribution to easing the social demand for higher education, accounting for up to 20 percent of enrollments in some countries. However, in many instances, there is a perception that the private institutions are profit-driven and therefore education offered by these institutions is inferior to that offered by pubic higher education institutions. The study did not find evidence to support this perception, especially because the staffing and state of facilities in some public tertiary institutions raise major doubts about the quality of education offered. A comprehensive quality assurance system could serve as a basis for comparing the quality offered in public and private institutions. This might in turn challenge public tertiary institutions to pay more attention to quality and also increase public confidence in private HE institutions, thus attracting more private investors into the higher education market.

### *Demands for Increased Transparency and Accountability*

Within public higher education institutions, student fees are becoming a significant contribution to recurrent budgets. At the University of Nairobi, student cost-sharing produced

37 percent of the institution's recurrent budget in 2002 (Kiamba 2003). In Ghana, student fees contributed 31 percent of university budgets in 2005 (Adu and Orivel 2006). At the recently-established University of The Gambia, student fees represented about 70 percent of overall expenditure in 2003/04 (University of The Gambia 2005). Countries such as Tanzania, Uganda and Zimbabwe are following suite. Although these cost-sharing schemes have often been met with student resistance, they have brought in needed funding to supplement insufficient government subventions. Resistance to cost-sharing is due in part to the lack of adequate mechanisms to ensure transparency in the use of resources and the relationship of these resources to the quality of outputs of HE institutions. An effective quality assurance system promotes transparency and accountability as institutions are required to open up to external scrutiny by peers, professional associations and national QA agencies where they exist. A good quality rating by external bodies is also likely to boost students' morale and commitment to their institution, possibly leading to increased readiness to contribute to the costs of their education. The argument for transparency and accountability is also one appreciated by the governments that must gain a better understanding of how their resources are being spent.

### *Need for Reforms in Tertiary Education to Address New Challenges*

Quality assurance can play a key catalytic role in initiating reforms to revitalize weak tertiary education systems. Despite variations in cultural and political preferences, differences in leadership styles within governments as well as varying stages of development, there is emerging consensus that traditional academic controls are inadequate for responding to today's challenges and that more explicit assurances about quality are needed (El-Khawas, DePietro-Jurand, and Holm-Nielsen 1998). Box 2 illustrates how Romania responded to the needs for change.

**Box 2: Lessons from Romanian Higher Education Reforms**

A 1994 education sector reform strategy introduced by the Romanian Government led to the 1995 Education Law. The new Law replaced centralized Ministry of Education (MOE) control with system oversight through intermediary councils of "buffer organizations." This was achieved by devolving professional and policy functions from the MOE to four, semiautonomous, intermediary councils: the National Council on Accreditation and Academic Evaluation, the National Council on Academic Titles and Degrees, the Higher Education Financing Council, and the University Research Council.

The higher education system is now more responsive to the needs of the emerging market economy. This has been accomplished by changing the content of programs, readjusting the size of programs, and building in more flexibility. New fields such as business and modern macro and micro-economics were introduced, while other fields, such as central planning, were eliminated. Over-specialization and over-enrollment in certain technical and engineering fields have been adjusted and interdisciplinary programs have been introduced. Flexibility has been increased through the introduction of short programs, retraining programs and continuing education.

In addition, revitalization of academic programs, through the Accreditation Council, is ensuring higher quality standards, especially in the newly developing public and private universities. Quality of faculty, in fast growing fields, is being upgraded through the development of postgraduate programs to train the next generation of academic staff, while the National Research Council is funding the development of new postgraduate programs and related research.

*Source:* World Bank (1996).

## *New Methods of Delivery Challenge Traditional Approaches to HE Development*

Recent advances in information and communication technologies (ICTs) have prompted changes in the modes of delivery for education. The use of different forms of Open and Distance Learning (ODL) is on the rise, making it possible to teach and learn from anywhere in the world irrespective of one's geographical location relative to the source of delivery. On-line education is growing, even within regular "brick and mortar" institutions. These new methods also render tertiary education "borderless"—students have options for access to higher education beyond their national boundaries and providers of HE can reach students anywhere in the world without having to secure clearance from any local authority. This is a positive development, especially for countries which cannot afford to invest in brick and mortar institutions (for example, small countries, weak economies) to meet the growing social demand. However, in the absence of an effective QA system, consumers lack a reliable basis for choosing between different borderless offers, and governments would not have a mechanism for holding these providers accountable for the quality of their programs.

In Africa this trend is expressed in the growing attention accorded to building capacities for distance education. The region now hosts four open universities, with plans to establish at least two more in the near future. Likewise, the provision of education "at a distance" by traditional universities is steadily expanding. In Tanzania, the Open University of Tanzania (OUT) is now the largest university in the country—only 15 years after its establishment. The African Virtual University which was initially incubated in the World Bank is now a well recognized leader in open and distance e-learning (ODEL) in Africa with a network that spans over 20 English and French-speaking countries. Though some familiarity with quality assurance processes for traditional (print-based) distance learning systems has been acquired on the continent, the new modes of delivery pose a challenge because there neither standards nor expertise are currently available to regulate quality.

## *Increasing Competition and Shorter Knowledge Cycles Require Continuous Improvement*

Tertiary education has become more competitive as a result of increasing private sector participation, growing demand for accountability, limited public funding for tertiary education, and the advent of borderless tertiary education. Competition in the developed world is forcing some institutions to seek new markets in developing countries. Some have established satellite campuses, or are partnering with local institutions in developing countries to offer their degree programs in areas that have ready markets, for example, business management and information technology. In view of the perceived greater recognition and marketability of foreign degrees, and the certainty of completing the degree within a prescribed period of time without the fear of interruption due to student crises, these 'name brand degrees' are becoming increasingly popular, posing a rising challenge for local universities in some countries. Added to this is the growing trend in international ranking of universities where hardly any African institutions appear among the top five hundred. With students and parents increasingly concerned about quality and ranking when selecting university degree programs (especially where payment of tuition is involved), African higher education institutions are likely to fall further behind if quality improvement is not given increased attention. An effective quality assurance system at institutional and national levels serves to continually monitor new knowledge creation and obliges institutions to regularly update curricula, teaching methods and learning approaches to ensure that their graduates have knowledge and skills relevant for current and future labor market needs.

### *Increasing Regional Collaboration Requires Harmonization of Qualifications and Awards*

Emerging regional economic blocks and the possibilities opened up by the inclusion of higher education in the General Agreement on Trade in Services (GATS), have prompted new regional and international initiatives to enhance student and workers mobility, while respecting individual countries' authority to regulate the quality of their own higher education systems. The Bologna process within the European Union is a good example.[7] Harmonization of study programs, qualifications and awards of tertiary institutions is also being pursued as a way to strengthen unity within the peoples of the regional block—a cohesion likely to have positive dividends to trade, peace, and security.

The effect of the Bologna process is being felt in Africa. Inspired by this initiative, the leads of state of six countries under the *Communaite Economique et Monataire de L'Afrique Centrale (CEMAC)*[8] decided in 2005 to adopt the *Licence, Master, Doctorat (LMD)* system in order to harmonize and standardize tertiary education systems in the subregion. Several additional Francophone countries have subsequently adopted the LMD system. The plan is to launch the *Licence* (equivalent to bachelors degree) in 2006/07, the *Masters* in 2007/08 and the *Doctorat* in 2009/10. Despite major capacity constraints, the transition to the LMD system is serving as a unifying factor that is likely to have a positive effect on regional collaboration among the countries involved. In addition, since the LMD system is very similar to the Anglophone higher education system, the change might facilitate increased collaboration and mobility between Francophone and Anglophone countries in Africa.

Other regions are making similar efforts. The Asia Pacific Region has established a quality assurance network—the Asia Pacific Quality Network (APQN)[9]—to promote mobility of students and skilled workers within the region. Latin America and the Caribbean (LAC) countries have also initiated their own network (RIACES). At the global level, the International Network for Quality Assurance Agencies in Higher education (INQAAHE) was established in 1991 to promote sharing of knowledge and experience in quality assurance. However, the strength of these networks can only be as strong as their constituent national quality assurance systems. Strengthening of national and institutional quality systems is therefore of critical strategic importance.

---

7. The Bologna Process was launched in 1999 to establish a common European Higher Education Area by 2010. Currently 45 countries participate. The goal is to facilitate student mobility among countries through harmonization of HE systems, to boost the attractiveness of European higher education, and to improve higher education quality for the development of Europe (www.coe.int/T/DG4/HigherEducation/EHEA2010/BolognaPedestrians_en.asp).

8. CEMAC member countries are: Cameroun, Central African Republic, Congo, Gabon, Equatorial Guinea and Chad. The declaration on the decision to introduce the LMD system was signed in February 2005 by the heads of state of these countries.

9. More information on the APQN can be obtained at www.apqn.org

In Africa, the higher education landscape is largely a product of the colonial history of the continent, post-independence socioeconomic stresses, and recent developments in delivery methods that have simplified cross-border delivery. The resulting effect is an interesting mosaic of diverse higher education systems divided along language lines (Anglophone, Francophone, Lusophone, and Arabophone), each with its own structure and a diverse array of study programs, qualifications and awards. Yet, in spite of these differences, common efforts are emerging to forge unity in the region through enhancement of access to higher education. Mutual recognition of qualifications and creating a common framework for credit-transfer have been agreed upon as one of the key pathways to promoting mobility across the educational systems of African countries[10]. A regional commitment to quality is also evident in the institutionalisation of quality assurance mechanisms for higher education in Africa.[11] A renewed focus on QA in higher education would raise awareness of this subject, while creating the capacity and incentive to participate in these regional initiatives.

### *Quality Higher Education in Africa Could Improve Retention of Skilled Human Capital*

Most emigrants are initially attracted abroad by the quality and status attached to tertiary institutions in those countries. But at the completion of their studies, too few return home to apply their newly acquired skills. Most worrisome is the fact that Sub-Saharan Africa (SSA), the poorest among the poor regions of the world, has the highest rate of emigration of skilled workers. The percentage of tertiary-educated emigrants from the region increased from 23 percent in 1990 to 31.4 percent in 2000 (Docquier and Marfouk 2005). This not only exacerbates the relative scarcity of key skills. More importantly, it demobilizes middle and lower level skills because of insufficient supervisory capacity.

Debate on the positive economic effects of skilled emigration (brain drain) on the sending countries remains inconclusive. Thus, assuming that other factors that influence migration choices remain constant, improving the quality of tertiary education in Africa would likely enhance the attractiveness of home institutions and consequently increase the number of qualified students that study in their home country institutions. This, in turn, might enhance the availability of highly skilled human capacity. It needs to be noted, however, that if QA is successful in achieving harmonization of degrees and competencies in the spirit of enhancing mobility as is the case with the Bologna Process, this achievement could fuel the migration of skilled labor.

## What Has Been Africa's Response to the Quality Challenge?

As elsewhere in the world, the quest for quality has always been a priority in higher education in Africa. Until recently, however, the tension between political pressure to expand access

10. The Arusha Convention enacted by African Heads of State in 1981 is a Regional Convention on the Recognition of Studies, Certificates Diplomas, Degrees and other Academic Qualifications in Higher Education in African States. It has yet to take off because a majority of states have yet to ratify it. The AAU plans to update it and seek wide ratification.

11. The AAU plans to launch a major initiative on regional collaboration in QA, possibly leading to the establishment of an African knowledge sharing network on Quality Assurance in Higher Education.

and the desire by academics in HEIs to maintain quality did not allow a healthy culture of quality to evolve. Changes in quality assurance mechanisms over the years were driven by factors such as rapid enrollment growth to meet increasing social demand, significantly decreased public funding of higher education amid rising enrollment, and the effects of the brain drain.[12] However, recent increases in private sector participation in tertiary education appears to have provided the trigger for governments, and to a less extent institutions, employers and the public, to give a greater attention to educational quality. An analytical review of developments in quality assurance in Africa, including current challenges and opportunities for capacity enhancement are discussed in the following sections.

12. The cost to South Africa for the brain drain in medicine to New Zealand in the mid-1990s was estimated to be 50 million rand. Personal communication of research findings: Daniel J. Ncayiyana, April 15, 2006. See also Saffu (2006), p. 15–16, regarding shortages and brain drain of professionals.

CHAPTER 3

# The State of Quality Assurance in Africa

## Brief History

### *Affiliation Was the First Form of QA in African Higher Education*

The history of quality assurance in higher education in Africa goes back to the founding of the first universities in Africa (for example, Fourah Bay College in Sierra Leone in 1827), all of which were affiliated to partner universities located in the colonizing countries (the United Kingdom, France, and Portugal). The University of Dakar, now Cheikh Anta Diop University in Senegal, was regarded as an integral part of the French higher education system as late as the 1960s. Authority over the quality of university education in those early days was a function of their governing boards and faculty. With affiliation, the institutions automatically became part of the British, French, Portuguese or other systems of quality assurance through their partner universities. These institutions were subject to the same kinds of quality control as were British or other European universities, including external examiners and other aspects of these systems.

As other new universities were established, some of them were also affiliated with external institutions. Over time, some of the first institutions, such as the University of Cape Town, became mentors for younger institutions in South Africa, as was the case for Fort Hare University which was affiliated with Rhodes University. Even with affiliation, a high degree of institutional autonomy was maintained. Thus, quality assurance was seen primarily as the province of the faculty and governance bodies at each university.

### *Increased State Authority After Independence Often Favored Access over Quality*

At independence the role of state authority over higher education increased. Most departments and ministries of education took an interest in the universities and asserted greater control over their governance and decision-making. That was not always done in support of quality. Indeed, in some cases, the increased role of the state in university education contributed to a decline in the quality of higher education as a desire for political control of education, appointments to management and governing bodies were made largely on political, rather than on merit, basis.

During the period immediately following independence, most ministries and departments of education were given legal authority and oversight over higher education, though the level of authority varied widely from one country to another.[13] Some governments established highly centralized authority over higher education (as in Cameroon, Nigeria, and Madagascar). Others granted high levels of autonomy to public and/or private education either by law or in fact (as in Guinea, Liberia, and the Congo; see Bloom, Canning, and Chan 2006). National governments had their own interests and priorities which were not always in accord with those of the universities. They included increased access, expectations of university contributions to the development of the nation, and in some cases, the desire to control political dissent which was often seen as originating in the universities.

### *The External Examiner System Gave Legitimacy and Credibility to Examination Results*

The external examiner system, where it existed, helped to ensure that academic programs and final examinations were reviewed on a regular basis by people committed to maintaining academic standards. In many universities, external examiners are given substantial power over final marks, and lend credibility and legitimacy to the final grades in the eyes of the students, the institution and the public. Even before the current drive for quality assurance, a few examples of accreditation of African universities by foreign accreditors were noteworthy. These include the University of Asmara in Eritrea in 1960 by the Superior Council of the Institute of Italian Universities and the University of South Africa (UNISA) by the Distance Education and Training Council, a United States distance education accreditor, in 1992.

Although the external examination system continued to provide a level of quality assurance in many countries well beyond the end of the colonial era—often using external examiners from neighboring African states—it began to weaken in the 1980s and 1990s. This was due to the growing size of the student populations and the resulting difficulties for effective external examination (the inability of external examiners to read all of the examinations in very large classes) and the high cost of the system itself with the increasing prices of air fares and lodging for growing numbers of examiners.

### *Decreasing Per Student Public Expenditure During the 1980s and 1990s Led to Decline in Quality*

The rapid growth in student enrollments at most higher education institutions in Africa during the 1980s and 1990s created additional problems. Higher education enrollments in Ghana, for example, grew from 11,857 in 1991/92 to 63,576 in 2003/2004, an increase of

13. For a very useful overview see Bloom, Canning, and Chan (2006), Appendices B and C which trace the growth of legal and practical authority of African governments of higher education.

over 400 percent.[14] Nigeria saw a tremendous expansion in the number of universities from six in 1970 to about 240 higher education institutions and an enrollment of over 1.5 million in 2006 (Okebukola 2006). This rapid growth had profound negative effects on the quality of teaching and learning (Jibril 2006). While the annual enrollment growth rate was rising, the average public expenditures per student in higher education fell significantly during most of this period with detrimental effects on quality.[15] This situation was exacerbated by inefficiencies in the system and funding policies that had little or no link to performance. Though Nigeria and some other governments have now taken measures to reverse this decline, it will take many years of sustained efforts to recover fully.

### *Pressure from Private Participation Triggered Setting of National QA Agencies*

Lacking robust mechanisms to regulate private tertiary providers, some governments began to face problems of educational quality stemming from the rapid growth of private higher education institutions in the 1990s. Problems cited include: unlicensed private institutions, unqualified academic staff, sub-standard curricula, and lack of essential facilities, for example, laboratories. At the same time, calls for a higher quality of graduates from employers, together with governments' recognition of the need to be competitive internationally and to meet the demands of knowledge societies, has fueled a recent debate on the need to set national benchmarks linked to world-class standards. As Daniel Ncayiyana (2006) notes:

> [H]igher education could no longer continue with "business as usual." The old collegial model of quality assurance could no longer be relied upon solely to ensure that the public was being well served, or that the taxpayer was getting value for money.

As a consequence, the higher education community, governments and other stakeholders sought new mechanisms to improve quality so as to halt the perceived decline in the quality of higher education. Because most departments and ministries of education had been given or assumed greater power over higher education, it is not surprising that they were the major force behind the establishment of new quality assurance structures. Over the years many of them had challenged university autonomy, showed much less deference to the universities and their faculty members than in the past, and insisted on greater control. In addition, some departments and ministries of education had became the focal point of higher education expansion both to meet the growing demand for access and to benefit from the political patronage that flowed from contracts for construction, equipment, supplies and other needs. These decisions were increasingly driven by politics rather than knowledge needs or the national capacity to support new higher education institutions. As the number of institutions rose, demands arose in some countries for these new higher education institutions to be dispersed geographically (for example, Nigeria and Ethiopia).

The period of rapid growth in higher education institutions was accompanied by one of general economic decline and austerity in most of Africa. This caused university budgets

14. Paul Effah (2004), "Private Higher Education in Ghana," as cited in Saffu (2006).

15. The higher education enrollment rates of low income countries grew an average of 8.8 percent in the 1990s while public expenditures fell 12.3 percent during the same period (World Bank 1994, p. 17).

shrink as they took their share of budget cuts or stagnating budgets amid increasing enrollments and rising inflation. In a number of countries, as in Nigeria, the decline in university quality was such that graduates increasingly had trouble obtaining employment even when jobs were available. The decline in quality, the growing internationalization of the professions in particular, recognition of the need to monitor an out-of-control private higher education sector, and a wide range of other concerns about higher education, contributed to the emergence of quality assurance agencies in a small number of countries. All were initiated by departments and ministries of education, often with the encouragement of university leaders and faculty members from both public and private higher education institutions. They too were eager to stem the decline and to foster a new era of quality and competitiveness for African higher education.

### *Francophone Africa Set Up the First Accreditation Body in SSA: CAMES*

The first formal accreditation processes in tertiary education took place in Francophone Africa in 1968 with the creation of the *Conseil Africain et Malgache pour l'Enseignement Superieur (CAMES)* to, among others, harmonize recognition and equivalence of awards among member nations.[16] Today, CAMES is also responsible for accrediting private universities as well as a select number of professional programs. Despite this early start, the rapid increase in student enrollments, the insufficiency of financial resources allocated to the higher education sector, and the implementation of policies which allocated a significant share of these resources to student scholarships and various subsidized social services resulted in a major decline in the relevance and quality of higher education offered in these countries during the 1970s and 1980s (Shabani 2006). Although some countries have, during the 1990s, undertaken some reforms to address this decline, the problems cited above continue to exist in most countries (Brossard and Foko 2006). In the 1980s, Anglophone Africa (Nigeria and South Africa) were the first to enter the arena of quality assurance, notably in technical education. Specifically, the National Board for Technical Education (NBTE) was created in Nigeria in 1981 and the Committee of Technikon Principals in South Africa in 1986.

### *The First National QA Agencies Were Set Up During the Quality Decline of the 1980s*

At the level of university education, the first national accreditation agency was established in Kenya by the Commission for Higher Education (CHE) in 1985 by an Act of Parliament. The CHE was set up because of "general concern" about the quality of higher education and the existence of several institutions offering "university education whose establishment and development was uncoordinated and unregulated. . ." (CHE 2006). Among its functions were accreditation and inspection of institutions of higher education. Standards for accreditation were established in 1989 along with rules for establishing new universities. The actual accreditation process began in 1989 in Kenya only for private universities.

16. The 16 member countries of CAMES are Benin, Burkina Faso, Burundi, Cameroon, Chad, Central African Republic, Congo, Gabon, Guinea, Ivory Coast, Madagascar, Mali, Niger, Rwanda, Senegal, and Togo.

Among the first to be accredited was the Catholic University of East Africa. Accreditation in Kenya now is required for private universities, new public universities, foreign universities and/or other agencies operating on their behalf (CHE 2006). Those established by Parliament continue to be accredited *de jure*.

Nigeria was the second of the pioneers in university-level accreditation in Africa. Its efforts took the form of program accreditation (not institutional accreditation). The first accreditation exercise was undertaken by the National Universities Commission (NUC) in 1990–91, 10 years after the first tertiary accreditation exercise in Nigeria by the National Board for Technical Education. The NUC was established in 1962 to provide oversight to the national higher education system. It was given accreditation responsibilities in the 1990s. A second round of program accreditation was carried out in 1999–2000 and a third was done in 2005. Notably, the 2005 accreditation exercise also included the ranking of universities using 12 performance indicators (Jibril 2006). The results attracted considerable attention by institutions, the public and employers.

Cameroon, Ghana, Tanzania and Mauritius established their quality assurance agencies between 1991 and 1997. For an initial period, all these agencies limited their activities to accreditation of private universities. In Cameroon, the process is carried out under the auspices of the National Commission on Private Higher Education (NCPHE), but the final decision on accreditation is made by the Minister of Higher Education. To date, only two private institutions have been fully accredited in Cameroon. Ghana instituted accreditation in 1993 with actual accreditation of polytechnics and private universities starting in 1996 and public universities in 2005. The Ghanaian National Accreditation Board accredits public, private, foreign, and distance education institutions. Tanzania has just changed the law to extend the mandate of its QA agencies to public tertiary institutions. Mauritius set up the quality assurance division of the Tertiary Education Commission (TEC) in 1997, but did not begin the process of quality audits and program accreditation until 2005. South Africa began preparation for higher education audits and accreditation with the establishment of the Higher Education Quality Committee (HEQC) of the Council for Higher Education (CHE) in September 2001.

## National QA Agencies: Mandates and Processes

### *Formal Quality Assurance Processes in Africa Are a Recent Phenomenon but the Situation is Rapidly Evolving*

The Appendix summarizes the status of QA in each of 52 African countries. Although about 25 countries practice some form of quality assurance process, only 30 percent of African countries (a total of 16) have established and operationalized quality assurance agencies. The countries with established quality assurance agencies (including CAMES) are shown in Table 1. Most were created within the last ten years, mainly in response to the documented decline in the quality of higher education in Africa during the 1980s and the resulting proliferation of private higher education. All but five of the agencies operate as semi-autonomous bodies with their own establishing law, governing board and budget allocation, and their decisions on accreditation are final. The rest are highly dependent on government; that is, their governance, management and financing are tightly controlled by

**Table 1. National Quality Assurance and Accreditation Agencies in Africa**

| Country | Agency | Date Established | Level of Autonomy |
|---|---|---|---|
| 16 Francophone Countries + Guinea Bissau | *Conseil Africain et Malgasche pour l'Ensignement Superieur* (CAMES) | 1968 | Semi |
| Kenya | Commission for Higher Education (CHE) | 1985 | Semi |
| Nigeria | National Universities Commission (NUC) | 1990 | Semi |
| Cameroon | National Commission on Private Higher Education (NCPHE) | 1991 | No |
| Ghana | National Accreditation Board (NAB) | 1993 | Semi |
| Tanzania | Higher Education Accreditation Council (HEAC) | 1995 | Semi |
| Tunisia | Comite National d'Evaluation (CNE) | 1995 | Semi |
| Mauritius | Tertiary Education Commission (TEC) | 1997 | Semi |
| Liberia | National Commission on Higher Education (NCHE) | 2000 | Semi |
| South Africa | Higher Education Quality Committee (HEQC) of the Council on Higher Education (CHE) | 2001 | Semi |
| Ethiopia | Higher Education Relevance and Quality Assurance Agency (HERQA) | 2003 | No |
| Mozambique | National Commission for Accreditation and Evaluation of Higher Education (CNAQ) | 2003 | Semi |
| Sudan | Evaluation and Accreditation Corporation (EVAC) | 2003 | No |
| Egypt | National Quality Assurance and Accreditation Committee (NQAAC) | 2004 | Semi |
| Namibia | National Council for Higher Education (NCHE) | 2004 | No |
| Uganda | National Council for Higher Education (NCHE) | 2005 | Semi |
| Zimbabwe | National Council for Higher Education (NCHE) | 2006 | No |

government and their decisions are subject to approval by the government (for example, Minister for Higher Education in Cameroon). Each of the accrediting agencies has its own board though the compositions differ. Some consist mostly of government officials and vice chancellors from the different universities while others incorporate a broad cross-section of universities, government, business, professionals, and the public.

A notable observation is that Francophone countries seem to lag behind Anglophone countries in establishing formal quality assurance processes at the national level. While the reasons for this are unclear, this is probably due to the assumption by governments that responsibility for QA has been assigned to CAMES. However, as concluded in a recent conference on Higher Education in Francophone Africa, quality remains a major concern in most Francophone countries, and it needs to be given high priority as an indispensable part of revitalizing higher education in these countries.

Several countries (Botswana, Madagascar, Tunisia, and Seychelles) are currently in the process of establishing quality assurance agencies. The Democratic Republic of Congo has

**Table 2. Legal Mandates of National QA Agencies in Case Study Countries, April 2006**

| Country | Cameroon | Ghana | Mauritius | Nigeria | S. Africa | Tanzania |
|---|---|---|---|---|---|---|
| **Mandates of National QA Agencies** | | | | | | |
| Assess institutions and/ or programs | x | x | x | x | x | x |
| Approval of new academic programs/courses | x | x | x | x | x | x |
| Approval of new higher education institutions | x* | x | x | x | x | x |
| Set minimum academic standards | x | x | x | x | x | x |
| Advise government re Visitations | | | | x | | |
| Rank institutions | | | | x | | |
| Annual performance/ monitoring | x | x | x | x | x | x |
| Recognition of degrees & equivalence | x | x | | | x | x |
| Oversee/evaluate transfers between institutions | | | | | | x |
| Approve admissions to institutions | | | | | | x |
| Standardization of academic designations & titles | | | | | | x |
| Equitable access: gender, race, region, econ. | | x | | | x | x |
| Monitor part-time staff levels | | | | | x | x |
| External examiners coordination | | | x | x | x | |
| Approve foreign institutions | x | x | x | x | x | x |

* Private institutions only. Public institutions considered accredited *de jure*.

asked for Bank assistance to strengthen its QA system. Zimbabwe recently passed legislation establishing a quality assurance agency.[17]

## Mandates

The legal mandates of national QA agencies in Africa have several similarities. All have authority to assess institutions and/or programs, approve new programs, and approve (or deny) the creation of new private tertiary institutions. As shown on Table 2, all of the agencies set minimum standards for institutions and/or programs, monitor the performance of

17. "Government Establishes Quality Assurance Agency," *The Herald*, February 18, 2006.

institutions reviewed, and have the power to approve or deny permission to operate to foreign institutions.

Perhaps reflecting the strong link between these agencies and government, some agencies also play the role of adviser to the government. In the case of Ghana, South Africa and Tanzania, the QA agencies are, in addition, responsible for ensuring equitable access to higher education irrespective of gender, race, religion or economic status—a function normally performed by the ministry itself. The national QA agency in Tanzania has the additional responsibility of approving admissions to HE institutions as well as for overseeing transfers between institutions—early signs of a move towards a national qualifications framework. In Nigeria, the QA agency is also responsible for ranking of HEIs as part of the accreditation process—a function usually undertaken by an independent body, separate from the accreditation process. This means that QA agencies at this early stage in Africa are responsible for multiple functions beyond those performed by a typical agency in more developed HE systems.

In countries without national QA agencies, the ministry or department responsible for higher education has legal authority over quality assurance and accreditation. However, there is little evidence of formal processes to carry out these functions. Typically, the power (for example, to accredit new private institutions) is vested in the minister responsible for higher education, with (or sometimes without) a specific supporting team to scrutinize applications and advise the minister. In Cameroon, for example, although an agency for accrediting private higher education is operative, the Minister for Higher education has tremendous powers over quality assurance and accreditation throughout the system. Box 3 illustrates the Cameroon case.

At a first glance, this arrangement might seem effective as it elevates the quality assurance function to a high level of decision-making. However, since ministerial positions are political in nature and often subject to high turnover, there could be problems of consistency leading to loss of credibility and trust in the system.

Except for Cameroon, all the countries with national QA agencies now cover both public and private institutions of higher learning (separate QA bodies exist for non-degree

**Box 3: Power of the Minister for Higher Education in Cameroon**

The Minister of Higher Education has direct supervisory authority over the six state universities where he ensures that academic standards and programmes are respected, approves new programmes and diplomas, appoints and dismisses the Heads of academic departments and programmes on advice of the Vice-Chancellor or Rectors and acts as Chancellor and Visitor at the state universities. The Minister of Higher Education presides over the National Commission on Private Higher Education (NCPHE) and approves or rejects proposals by the NCPHE to accredit private institutions. The Minister of Higher Education also has the power and responsibility to approve study syllabuses in both public and private higher education institutions. The Minister of Higher Education is represented on the Councils or Boards of all state universities and the majority of state institutions of higher learning under the supervision of other ministries. This representation allows him to give an opinion on the quality of the study programmes of these institutions. As chairperson of the National Equivalence Board (NEB) the Minister of Higher Education recognises foreign schools, certificates and programmes on the advice of the NEB.

*Source:* Titanji (2006).

granting tertiary institutions). Although it is too early to conclude how this mandate will be received by staff and management in public institutions, limited experience from Nigeria indicates that the practice is likely to strengthen the credibility of private higher education institutions which have in most countries been regarded as delivering inferior education. In the 2005 program accreditation of Nigerian universities, none of the private universities reviewed had a program rejected while 6 major public universities had at least one program rejected.

## QA Processes

### *Despite Differences in the Mandates of National Agencies, Activities of These Agencies Are Remarkably Similar*

Table 3 gives an overview of accreditation and audit activities in the six case study countries. Although the agencies in these countries are at very different levels of development, a convergence in the QA processes seems apparent. They all perform the same set of processes and go through similar stages in accrediting or auditing a program or an institution: self-assessment, peer review, site visit, and a written report. In the case of Cameroon, the self-study is in the form of a detailed application package. These processes are similar to those followed by agencies in other regions. This seems to reflect a general trend in African

**Table 3. QA Processes and Stages in National Agencies of Case Study Countries, April 2006**

| Country | Cameroon | Ghana | Mauritius | Nigeria | S. Africa | Tanzania |
|---|---|---|---|---|---|---|
| **QA Processes** | | | | | | |
| Peer Reviews | x* | x | x | x | x | x |
| Institutional Self-assessments | *** | x | x | x | x | x** |
| Site Visits | x | x | x | x | x | x |
| Report | x | x | x | x | x | x |
| **Stages of Accreditation** | | | | | | |
| 1. Permission to apply | | | | | | x |
| 2. Provisional Registration/ Authorization | x | x | | x | x | x |
| 3. Registration | x | x | | | | x |
| 4. Approval for Candidacy for Accreditation | x | x | | | x | |
| 5. Accreditation | x | x | x-prog. | x | x-prog. | x |
| 6. Reaccreditations (every 4–6 years) | x | x | x | x | x | x |

x-prog. Program accreditation only.
* Includes academic and Ministry officials.
** Optional until 2005.
*** Institution submits detailed application.

universities to strive to conform to international standards, in most cases drawing from standards in the developed (OECD) countries. As discussed later in the report, though there is nothing wrong with this desire, financial cost and limited human resource capacity are main constraints that inhibit full-scale deployment of quality assurance processes in Africa. Perhaps African countries need to reconsider their approach to quality assurance and adopt approaches commensurate with available capacity.

### *Successful Development of Standards and Criteria for Accreditation Requires Broad Consultations*

The standards for accreditation and the criteria for candidacy for accreditation and audits have been the subject of extensive discussion in the countries that currently undertake accreditation and audits. Interviews conducted indicate that most national agencies developed their standards through a highly consultative process. Draft documents were widely circulated and stakeholders were encouraged to give feedback before the standards were put in place. The agencies studied demonstrated a deep respect for the need to exercise great care, engage in consultations, and pilot the standards before full deployment. In the cases of Egypt[18] and Mauritius,[19] the agreed standards and criteria are published on the worldwide web. The consultative process in South Africa during development of criteria and standards proved to be especially effective in fostering agreement and legitimacy for the process. Despite these consultations, interviews in the case study countries revealed significant complaints and fears among academic staff in HEIs (for example, see South Africa case study) when these standards were actually applied. This underscores the critical importance of a robust communication strategy in implementing QA processes, particularly where external reviews or site visits are involved.

Standards set by quality assurance agencies vary in their scope but commonly exhibit insufficient appreciation of the link between these standards and funding as well as the needs of the labor market and the community. All the case study countries have standard requirements for the following common elements: mission, academic programs, faculty and staff quality, library and information resources, infrastructure, and finances (see Table 4). Several included standards for governance, internal quality assurance processes, integrity, and planning.

A key observation is the apparent lack of appreciation by many countries of the link between institutional governance, community service, and relations with industry on one hand, and with quality on the other. As Table 4 shows, half of the case study countries do not include governance as one of the standards and only a third indicate a link to community service and the work place as important. This is worrisome because the governance of an institution has a direct link to financing, accountability, responsiveness, and academic autonomy, which together have an impact on the quality of learning.

Flexibility and consultations in defining standards are key to successful implementation. Many of the standards reviewed during the study employ terms such as "appropriate to" or "suitable conditions for" or facilities that are "adequate for" the specific needs. The vagueness

18. Guidelines and templates for internal quality assurance system in higher education institutions. www.qaap.net/doc/puplications/Support%20moni/QAAP%20management%20&%20monitoring%20manual,%20final.doc

19. Tertiary Education Commission of Mauritius: http://tec.intnet.mu/quality.htm

**Table 4. Standards Used in Accreditation and Audits: Case Studies, April 2006**

| | Cameroon | Ghana | Mauritius | Nigeria | South Africa | Tanzania |
|---|---|---|---|---|---|---|
| Mission and purpose | X | X | X | X | X | X |
| Planning and evaluation | | X | X | | X | X |
| Governance | | X | | | X | X |
| Academic programs | X | X | X | X | X | X |
| Staff—quality, research, teaching, service | X | X | X | X | X | X |
| Students—recruitment, resources, learning | | X | X | X | X | X |
| Library and information resources | X | X | X | X | X | X |
| Physical and technological resources | X | X | X | X | X | X |
| Finances | X | X | X | X | X | X |
| Integrity | | X | | | X | X |
| Quality assurance mechanisms | | X | X | | X | X |
| National development or community service | | | X | | X | |
| Industrial links or work-based experience | | X | X | | | |

of these standards leaves them open to subjective interpretation and undoubtedly puts a great deal of pressure on the peer reviewers to make judgments about what is reasonable. This in turn might cast doubt on the legitimacy of the outcome of the process. Nonetheless, most people interviewed seemed to accept that such relative standards were essential and were far preferable to those which prescribed specific minimum levels such as a prescribed percentage of PhDs in the faculty or the number of books per subject in the library. The debate on accreditation of MBA programs in South Africa demonstrated this difficulty. In many cases, the review panels had difficulty agreeing about what would be the appropriate level of compliance. Nonetheless, leaving such decisions to panels of peer reviewers seems to have worked well in practice. It also provides flexibility so that standards do not have to be revised too frequently and allows for changes in benchmarks as well as in definitions of what is regarded as "world-class" or "state-of-the-art" at any given point in time.

In sum, the two key lessons concerning standards are (i) the importance of extensive consultations with stakeholders, and (ii) the need for flexibility in defining and interpreting standards. Ultimately, the credibility of the results will rely significantly on the strength and integrity of the peer reviewers and the QA agency staff; hence the critical importance of adequate human capacity.

### *Most Countries Focus on Institutional Accreditation and Audits*

Most of the currently active quality assurance agencies in Africa focus on institution-level (rather than program-level) quality assurance. Eight of the 12 agencies reviewed carry out institutional accreditation and three (Mauritius, South Africa, and Tanzania) undertake audits. The one exception is Nigeria which carries out only program accreditation, and also ranks institutions.[20] The processes involved in institutional audits are very similar to those applied in institutional accreditation and include: self assessments, peer reviews, site visits, and a written report. The assessments in both cases involve judgments about quality, capacity, outcomes, and the need for improvement. Both accreditation and audits require a substantial amount of time to carry out effective self-assessments (often 12 to 18 months), the use of peer reviewers, site visits, reporting requirements, and follow-up. Both are costly in terms of travel, board and lodging for site visits, administrative and faculty time for self-studies and site visits, and administrative time for preparation of data and follow-up. The level of resource needs (discussed in more detail below), appears to be about the same in both processes. The critical difference is the use in accreditation of standards set nationally versus standards set by the institution itself and assessed by external reviewers in audits.

Why than do institutions choose one or the other? It would seem to depend on an institution's readiness to open up to external scrutiny. Institutional accreditation is better understood than institutional audits, and thus has greater international currency. Despite this fact, institutions like the University of Dar es Salaam in Tanzania tend to prefer starting with audits before exposing themselves to accreditation as a way to prepare for the more rigorous external scrutiny.[21]

### *Program Accreditation is Labor-intensive and Costly*

Two of the 12 countries with established QA agencies carry out program accreditation and several others plan to do so. Some countries intend to review and accredit all programs—as do both Nigeria and South Africa, although only Nigeria has actually implemented this resolve. Some have adopted a more limited approach focusing on the professions only. For many countries, that decision is based on recognition of the magnitude of the task involved in requiring accreditation of all programs (in most countries more than 100 programs exist at higher education levels). Remarkably, Nigeria accredited 1,343 programs in 48 universities and 5 colleges in 2005 (NUC 2006). Mindful of cost concerns, Madagascar has decided to carry out program accreditation as part of institutional accreditation, looking at a representative sample of programs during each accreditation cycle and establishing a schedule to insure that all are eventually reviewed.[22] Nigeria also undertakes a ranking of institutions as part of program accreditation. The key observation here is that as countries gather experience in these processes, some innovative approaches are beginning to evolve. Given the existing constraints in resources, innovations to enhance cost-effectiveness and impact are urgently needed.

---

20. As noted elsewhere, in at least three of these countries (Cameroon, Kenya, and Uganda), public universities are called "accredited" *de jure* but do not go through the processes of self-study, peer review, site visit, and so forth. The situation is, however, changing for example, in Uganda, Tanzania, and Ghana.

21. The University of Dar es Salaam in Tanzania has conducted two audits, one in 1998 and a follow-up in 2003. The University is now due for accreditation. To read more about the audits, go to www.worldbank.org/afr/teia: *Tertiary Education Reforms in Africa: Things That Work, 2003.*

22. This is the plan in Madagascar, for example. Madagascar is currently developing its quality assurance system.

### *A Majority of QA Agencies Also Do Evaluation and Recognition of Foreign Credentials*

Four out of the six case study QA agencies are also responsible for recognizing foreign academic credentials and determining their national equivalence. In all cases, the process seeks to establish the authenticity of the awarding institution, the entry requirements, evidence of admission into the program, scope of the curriculum, course duration, contact hours per course, qualifications of academic staff at the awarding institution, the mode of delivery used by the institution, and certified true copies of the applicant's transcript and certificates awarded. Evaluation is conducted by a team appointed by the QA agency. This evaluation forms the basis for decision. The quality of this evaluation inevitably depends on the strength of the team and their knowledge of various HE systems globally—an area that requires strengthening in most QA agencies.

### *Ranking of Institutions by QA Agencies is Emerging and the Public is Paying Attention*

Only Nigeria ranks programs and institutions as part of the accreditation process. Program ranking started with its first program accreditation review in 1990/91. Program ranking was subsequently aggregated into a ranking of all Nigerian public universities using what were called the *mean academic quality index* scores which resulted from aggregating the ranking of individual programs (NUC 2002). A more comprehensive ranking system at the institutional level was used in 1999/2000 and in 2005, employing a combination of scores from program accreditation rankings and eleven other variables namely: percentage of academic programs with full accreditation status, compliance with enrollment guidelines, proportion of academic staff who are full professors, proportion of foreign academic staff, proportion of foreign students, proportion of academic staff with outstanding academic achievements, internally generated revenue, research output, student completion and drop-out rates, PhD output, stability of university calendar, and student to personal computer ratio (Jibril 2006). The ranking has been very contentious in Nigeria. It has, however, helped employers make judgments about the quality of graduates and has focused the energies of many universities on improving the quality of low-ranked programs as a means of elevating their ranking.

Overall, experience with ranking has mixed results.[23] Even the best of systems is arbitrary in many respects in terms of the weight given to different factors (for example, quality of laboratory equipment) or the mix of teaching to support staff (which surely varies by type of program). This may lead institutions to plan academic programs based on the way ranking is scored rather than on academic and labor market needs.

Despite these methodological problems, it would seem that ranking is here to stay as more and more countries are becoming interested in ranking, either as an international comparator for their national higher education system or to catalyze reform and innovations

23. Pakistan carried out a ranking exercise that took over a year to prepare and substantial resources. The Higher Education Commission was so dissatisfied with the results that the rankings were not released. A ranking of institutions carried out by Centre for Higher Education Transformation and a local newspaper in South Africa, though published, was so unsatisfactory that participants and the higher education institutions abandoned it after doing it once.

locally (Liu and Cheng 2005 and Newsweek 2006). For African institutions, these rankings present a major challenge because the public associates ranking with quality of education even though the indicators used are more inclined towards research quality and output. For example, according to the 2005 Shanghai Jiao Tong University worldwide rankings, only five African HEIs appear in the top 500 (4 from South Africa and 1 from Egypt). This compares poorly not only with developed countries but also with other developing regions like the Asia/Pacific region which listed 92 universities in the top 500.[24] Even if the population factor is taken into account, this is still a dismal comparison. A likely explanation could be the limited availability of published and internationally comparable data on African HEIs since these global rankings are based on publicly available information on academic and research performance. For example, rankings by Shanghai Jiao Tong University are derived using public information on research output as measured through published articles and citations (40 percent), highly cited researchers (20 percent), staff winning Nobel Prize and Fields Medals (20 percent), alumni winning Nobel Prize and Field Medals (10 percent), and size of an institution (10 percent). Thus, for African HEIs to improve their international standing, quality improvement has to go beyond quality assurance within institutions and by national agencies to include strategies to ensure that academic and research outputs are published in internationally recognized media.

### *Sanctions are Effective but Incentives for Compliance are Insufficient*

Table 5 presents a summary of the accreditation decisions made so far (April 2006) by respective QA agencies in nine countries. All but one of the agencies have either denied accreditation or put institutions on probation in specific cases. The exception, Tanzania, has a formative process that is incremental, with those not meeting the conditions for accreditation having the opportunity to meet the requirements at a later date, in some cases with restrictions on their ability to admit new students.[25] Sanctions imposed for not meeting the standards differ from country to country. In Nigeria, for example, programs that partially meet the requirements are given a specific period of time during which they are required to improve the quality of these programs, failing which the programs would be terminated. Failing programs are required to stop admitting new students immediately but pipeline students are allowed to complete their studies. It is too early to judge how these actions ultimately affect the relevance of education to the labor market since these processes have only been applied for a short time. Anecdotal information from Nigeria suggests that employers and students are beginning to pay attention to the results of QA processes in making their respective choices to hire or join an institution. Yet despite these positive signals, no formal linkage can yet be found between the results of quality assurance reviews and public funding decisions.

Incentives for compliance are weak and in some cases lacking. Except in Nigeria where institutions whose programs are found partially deficient are given priority in applications

24. 2005 World Ranking of Universities by the Institute of Higher Education, Shanghai Jiao Tong University—ARWU 2005 Statistics: http://ed.sjtu.edu.cn/rank/2006/ARWU2006Statistics,htm

25. For a full discussion of the four stages of the accreditation process see the case study by Mihyo (2006).

**Table 5. Summary of Accreditation Decisions in Nine Countries**

| | Institutional Accreditation/Audit | | | Program Accreditation | | |
|---|---|---|---|---|---|---|
| Country | Accredited | On Probation | Not Accredited | Accredited | On Probation | Not Accredited |
| Cameroon | x** | | x | x | | x |
| Ethiopia | | x | | NA | NA | NA |
| Ghana | x | x | x | x | x | x |
| Kenya | x** | x | x | NA | NA | NA |
| Mauritius | x* | x | | x | | x |
| Nigeria | NA | NA | NA | x | x | x |
| South Af | x* | NA | NA | x | | x |
| Tanzania | x*** | | | x | | |
| Uganda | x** | NA | x | x**** | | |

* Institutional audits—no judgment on accreditation or probation.
** Public institutions accredited *de jure.*
*** Public institutions originally *de jure;* accreditation underway.
**** Program accreditation mandated December 2005 and is forthcoming.

for funding under the Education Tax Fund,[26] very few countries have put in place formal mechanisms for assisting institutions to improve quality. One of the most successful approaches in other regions has been use of competitive funds for quality improvement. In this, Chile represents a good example (see Box 4).

## *Evidence Suggests That Accreditation Is Beginning to Catalyze Quality Improvement*

A question that is often asked is whether or not accreditation necessarily results in quality improvement. Although experience is currently limited, evidence from the Ghana, Nigeria, South Africa, and Tanzania case studies suggests it does. In both Ghana and Tanzania, reports obtained during the study indicate that institutions anticipating accreditation take measures to meet the standards for accreditation (for example, increasing computer access in one private institution) and take follow-up action in response to the decisions taken. The University of Dar es Salaam and the Muslim University of Morogoro (MUM) in Tanzania are examples of positive responses to accreditation reviews (Mihyo 2006). In South Africa, the process of preparing for self-assessments also encouraged institutions to improve quality to meet standards.[27] In the Ghana case study, Saffu (2006) notes that: "The

26. The Education Tax Fund (ETF) is a trust fund established in 1993 by the Government of Nigeria with the objective of improving the quality of education in Nigeria. All corporations and companies of identified minimum operating capacity and registered in Nigeria contribute a levy of 2 percent of their annual assessable profits to the Fund which complements Federal, State and Local Government budgets for the three levels of education nationwide.

27. Interviews with self-study team for the University of Pretoria, March 9, 2006.

### Box 4: Competitive Fund for Quality Improvement in Chile

The Higher Education Quality Improvement Program (MECESUP) set up a "competitive fund" in 1999 to promote quality and relevance in the higher education sub-sector through provision of grants to undergraduate and graduate programs in areas of institutional and national priority; and for improving facilities, equipment and human resources in institutions. Eligible expenditures included human resources development (scholarships for graduate studies in country and overseas; in-country postdoctoral work, visiting scholars and short visits abroad); goods (laboratory equipment, teaching and learning tools and ICTs); and buildings (improving academic space and environment). Institutions selected what was to be funded under the project based on institutional strategic plans and national priorities. The competition was repeated in 2001.

*Source:* Robin De Pietro and Maria Jose Lemaitre (2002).

newer tertiary institutions that have sprung up to meet the strong demand for tertiary education are forced by the existence of NAB to be seriously mindful of quality assurance. If they want accreditation they have no choice but to tow the NAB line on quality assurance. The NAB requires them to establish Quality Assurance Units and affiliate to an existing established university for an initial period, and for purposes of mentoring." He concludes: "NAB is helping to keep in check the entrepreneurs who would have had a field day, unleashing a whole stream of useless but lucrative tertiary institutions to meet the undoubted demand that exists for tertiary qualifications and certificates." In the case study of Tanzania, Mihyo cites several concrete changes growing out of the quality assurance and accreditation process (see Box 5). Another indication of acceptance of the outcomes is the fact that in only two instances have the six case studies reported that institutions challenged the decisions of the accrediting agency.

### Box 5: Contributions of Tanzanian Quality Assurance and Accreditation

The contributions of quality assurance and accreditation in Tanzania included:

- Program validation which has reduced discrepancies between programs offered locally and those offered abroad.
- Institutional visitation and physical inspection have reduced the potential problem of makeshift universities.
- Regulation of admission procedures has helped to reduce the potential for lowering of standards in admission.
- Regulation of promotions and recruitment procedures reduces the problems of sub-standard senior staff in universities.
- Control of use of part-time staff in universities helps to ensure those who teach have time for research.
- Evaluation and validation of credentials obtained from outside the country has reduced discrepancies between local and internationally recognized qualifications.
- Regulation of teaching resources by setting minimum standards helps to maintain the minimum required in terms of human and other resources for an institution to run higher education courses.

*Source:* Mihyo (2006), pp. 26–27.

## Quality Assurance within HE Institutions

Quality assurance within institutions of higher learning takes place throughout the teaching and learning process. It includes screening of candidates for admission, staff recruitment and promotion procedures, curriculum reviews, teaching and learning facilities, quality of research, policy development and management mechanisms, student evaluation of staff, external examiners for end-of-semester or end-of-year examinations, tracer studies, academic reviews and audits. Though little information is available in the public domain on the effectiveness of these methods, anecdotal information collected during this study indicates that implementation of some of these processes is weak due to financial constraints, failure to keep up with new approaches to teaching and learning (for example, ICTs), and increased workload resulting from large student numbers. In Tanzania, for example, a quality assurance panel set up by the University of Dar es Salaam (UDSM) recommended a reduction in the frequency of external examiner visits from once per year to once in two or three years. As a replacement, regular tracer studies were recommended to obtain feedback from the labor market (Mihyo 2006). Box 6 summarizes the recommendations of the Tanzania QA panel.

Because most of these processes are optional (not enforced by an external body), HEIs make adjustments (for example, reducing the frequency of or eliminating external examination) on an ongoing basis to adjust to cost and workload constraints as observed in the case of the University of Dar es Salaam. With guaranteed demand and *de jure* accreditation earned by virtue of their being public institutions, public HEIs are likely to allow trade-offs in quality to accommodate the social demand for access and to offset the effects of reduced funding from government instead of confronting the challenge of searching for alternative solutions. External QA systems when properly implemented can act as a deterrent to this shortcoming.

**Box 6: Findings of the UDSM Academic Audit Panel on Quality Assurance**

On quality assurance the panel focused on student evaluation, professionalism of staff, tracer studies and review of curricula, external examiners, admission criteria, annual staff review and staff recruitment. On student evaluation of teaching, the panel was of the opinion that although it had been used for decades, it was too routine and less objective. It recommended a new system that could ensure objectivity. On staff professionalism, it was recommended that teaching courses should be given to all teaching staff on regular bases. On external examiners, the panel found the system to be faulty due to excessive workload. It also found that the system was very expensive. It recommended use of external examiners every two or three years. Although tracer studies were conducted on regular basis by some faculties, the panel felt that the system was still optional. It recommended the exercise must be more regular and compulsory for all faculties.

On staff recruitment procedures, the panel noted there were some gaps and overlaps in various programmes. It was also noted that teaching was not given enough weight in decisions on promotions. It was recommended teaching methodology as well as ICT courses should be offered more regularly to all staff and teaching should be given some weight in the incentive systems.

*Source:* Mihyo (2006).

### *The Need for the External Examiner System Is Being Challenged, Given Existing Funding Problems and Emergence of External Accreditation by National Agencies*

As explained in the previous section, the external examiner system has been in existence in African higher education for more than fifty years. In the absence of a formal accreditation mechanism, this serves as an independent peer review mechanism which ensures that the programs being offered are equivalent to those in other tertiary institutions, and that the standards being applied are consistent with international practice. External examination looks neither into the way an institution is managed nor into the teaching and learning processes as this occurs at the end of the academic semester/year. The underlying assumption is that external examiners selected are themselves of high quality and are familiar with international standards and practices in the areas they examine. Over the last two decades, its implementation has become problematic due to cost and workload constraints, and several adjustments have been made. In places like Sokoine University in Tanzania, external examination has been replaced by an internal academic committee except for veterinary science where it is required by the respective professional body. Despite these shortcomings, external examination continues to be widely practiced in Sub-Saharan Africa. However, it is gradually being replaced by program and institutional reviews where external QA agencies have been established.

For the majority of countries which cannot afford a fully fledged external QA system, questions are being posed as to whether the limited funds available should be used for implementing a weak external examiners system (few examiners, limited to academics from neighboring countries, reduced number of days, many courses and students per examiner) or rather, it should be used for improving the quality of teachers and teaching facilities. The United Kingdom has used the external examiner system very effectively for decades and continues to do so with some of their institutions ranked among the best in the world. The difference, however, is that UK institutions implement very rigorous external examiner systems that are part of a university's strategic vision, with detailed guidelines and accompanied by through follow-up action, monitoring and evaluation.[28] There is, therefore, no single solution that fits all cases; each institution must assess its own situation against the resources available and select an appropriate method. Important, however, is to ensure that the quality assurance method selected is, itself, implemented with quality.

### *Institutional Academic Reviews Are Increasingly Being Undertaken by Institutions, Especially as Preparation for External Peer Review*

Institutional academic reviews are a more recent mechanism for quality assurance practiced in a few of the countries reviewed. It is a process undertaken by each institution on its own and not necessarily part of a national quality assurance process. The study found evidence of institutional academic reviews in less than 20 per cent of the 52 countries in sub-Saharan Africa. The number could be higher since little is currently published regarding institutional

---

28. The City University of London Code of Practice for External Examining, for example, specifies one external examiner for each degree program to serve for a maximum of five years. Each examiner produces a report annually, a summary of which is published as part of the National Teaching Quality dataset. and serves as a public reference on standards and quality.

QA processes. Countries with evidence of academic reviews as part of the quality assurance process are: South Africa, Cameroon, Ghana, Kenya, Mauritius, Nigeria, Tanzania, and Uganda. An academic review provides an opportunity for an institution to:[29]

- review an academic program or unit's mission and goals;
- evaluate the quality of the academic program, its faculty, staff, and students;
- establish priorities to develop its curriculum and to improve quality;
- determine the financial and material resources needed to support the university's and the unit's essential goals, and objectives;
- make recommendations for action by the program, the administration, and others;
- provide information that is essential to quality assessment, the development and the enhancement of the impact and reputation of the program and the university; and
- encourage units to be self-conscious about quality and its improvement.

The academic review process usually involves a self-study by the unit covering its programs, successes, weaknesses, and needs. The review is undertaken by a committee established for that purpose. This committee is normally made up of peers in related fields, at least one person from another disciplinary area, and sometimes an external member from another institution and/or the community. The review process usually includes an examination of: curriculum quality; workforce criteria (for example, student/staff ratios, teaching and research output); budget resources; quality of students and faculty; output criteria (for example, quality of students graduated; employment data, satisfaction of employers); efficiency criteria; (for example, pass through rate, first year failure rates); teaching quality (for example, peer evaluation of teaching quality, student evaluations of teaching quality); research output; service output; and contributions.

The study identified three main reasons why institutions undertake academic reviews:

- *As part of a broader reform program by an institution.* Even before external accreditation of public institutions became mandatory in Tanzania (2005), the University of Dar es Salaam undertook an academic review in 1998 as part of its Institutional Transformation Program aimed at revitalizing the institution following the decline of the 1980s. Kwame Nkrumah University of Science and Technology (KNUST) in Ghana undertook a similar exercise in 1999.
- *As preparation for external accreditation.* This is a necessary first step prior to external visitation by an accreditation team. Nigerian and South African HEIs have done this for several years and, following changes in the law to make external accreditation of public HEIs mandatory in Ghana, Tanzania and Uganda, similar reviews are being undertaken in those countries.
- *In response to a scandal that impinges upon an institution's academic integrity.* The University of Ghana, for example, conducted an academic review in 2005 in response to a scandal involving examination malpractices.

---

29. Based on work done for the American Council on Education (ACE) on Academic Program Reviews and a related series of workshops by Dr. Fred M. Hayward, Senior Associate, Prof. Donald W. Crawford, University of California Santa Barbara, Dr. Robert C. Shirley, University of Southern Colorado, and material provided by Dean Judith Aikin, Dean of Liberal Arts, University of Iowa.

**Box 7: Institutional Academic Review in Ghana**

The Kwame Nkrumah University of Science and Technology (KNUST) in Kumasi, along with Cape Coast University, have the best established and most effective Quality Assurance Units among all the tertiary institutions in the country. The KNUST Unit is not that old. It was established only in October 2002. There are several reasons for its effectiveness. First, it is combined with Planning. Its full name is the Quality Assurance and Planning Unit. Secondly, the Vice-Chancellor has taken a very keen, personal interest in the work of the Unit. In fact, the Unit is located in the offices of the Vice-Chancellor. Third, its Founding Coordinator is an inspirational, hardworking Professor whose enthusiasm for the work of his Unit is truly infectious. Finally, perhaps the most important reason, the Coordinator's approach to quality assurance and improvement, hence the Unit's as well, is holistic. Even healthy living, regular physical exercise and medical tests by staff and students, appear to qualify as aspects of quality assurance and improvement, perhaps reflecting the Latin dictum, *"Mens sana . . . ."*

Although program review has occupied a prominent position in the work of the Unit, as part of a radical restructuring of the organization of the University's numerous Faculties into just six Colleges, with a very substantial decentralization of decision-making to go with it, the activities of the Unit have encompassed: the introduction of regular staff assessment by students; the organization of capacity-building workshops for staff; a survey to determine the standard of teaching facilities at KNUST; the launching of Quality Assurance Management as a mainstream idea, through the organization of Staff, Student and Workers' Fora; the publication and distribution of Statutory Directives on Quality Assurance; and the publication and distribution of Quality Assurance Bulletins. A paper by the Coordinator, *"Management of Quality Assurance at KNUST—Summary Report on the Activities and Plans of the Quality Assurance and Planning Unit"* (September 2005), gives details of these activities.

*Source:* Saffu (2006), pp. 16–17.

A cross-cutting feature in all the institutions that have conducted academic reviews is the need for an *Academic Quality Assurance Unit* within the institution to manage implementation of the recommendations of the review, to ensure regular follow-up reviews, and to foster *a culture of quality* within the institution.

Academic reviews at HEIs can produce significant results in a relatively short time. For example, the Kwame Nkrumah University of Science and Technology (KNUST) in Ghana, which had been in a downward spiral for some time, was turned around after it carried out an extensive academic review of the overall institution (see Box 7). Self-assessment also generates a major capacity building dividend. First, it empowers the institution and its staff to take ownership of the quality function in their institution without pressure from an external body. Secondly, it helps institutions to identify their own strengths and weaknesses and to generate awareness on key performance indicators among staff. Thirdly, it is relatively inexpensive when compared to institutional or program accreditation. In brief, it helps institutions to build capacity from within. This capacity-building function of self-assessment is particularly important in the countries of Sub-Saharan Africa where capacity remains very weak.

A similar conclusion was reached by the University of Dar es Salaam, which has so far conducted two reviews (the University uses the term 'academic audit' for what is essentially a review). It now has instituted a policy of conducting reviews every five years. According to UDSM, academic reviews spur improvement and accountability in flexible and inexpensive ways. Academic staff can discuss education quality processes without the

**Box 8: Steps towards Establishment of a QA System at the University of Mauritius**

The University of Mauritius started putting in place a quality assurance system in the mid-1990s in parallel with efforts to set up a national Tertiary Education Commission. Highlights of the system are:

- QA is located under the Pro-Vice Chancellor for Curriculum Development.
- The university undertook broad consultations and obtained guidance from a number of foreign resource persons.
- A Strategic Plan (1999-2004) was then prepared, incorporating a QA strategy.
- A review of all academic processes was subsequently initiated.
- A University Quality Assurance Team (UQAT) was set up under the Senate with sub-teams in faculties and a special team for administrative matters.
- The outcomes of the review were documents detailing procedures, questionnaires, evaluation forms and templates for conducting QA assessments at various levels.
- A quality assurance office with a full-time director was appointed in 2002.
- External Audit was conducted by the Tertiary Education Commission in 2005.

*Source:* Mohamedbhai (2006).

defensiveness associated with direct quality evaluation. Because review discussions do not require expertise in any particular discipline, staff from all fields can learn and spread exemplary practices (Ishumi and Nkunya 2003).

Although many institutions claim to pay attention to quality issues, few actually have in place dedicated units that can monitor performance and advise management on a regular basis. In most cases, the assumption is that senior academic management (Deputy Vice Chancellor Academic, deans, heads of departments and respective university committees) hold responsibility for this function. However, with existing capacity constraints, these managers face overwhelming administrative demands for their attention and have little time left for other things. For this reason, HEIs that have undertaken internally driven academic reviews (for example, Ghana, Mauritius and Tanzania) encounter the need for a systematic approach to quality assurance managed by a dedicated administrative entity. Box 8 illustrates the line of attack taken by the University of Mauritius.

Three valuable lessons arise from the Mauritius example. First, it is important that quality assurance be part of the institution's strategic plan. Such plans should be developed through an all-inclusive consultative process in order to ensure broad ownership. Secondly, institutions need to assign responsibility for managing quality assurance to a specific unit that can implement quality improvement initiatives. Thirdly, for external QA processes to be meaningful, an institution needs to prepare itself well—sensitizing staff, conducting self-reviews, establishing the required institutional structures—well before the external process begins. Ultimately, the success of external QA processes depends upon how well institutions manage their internal QA systems.

## The Role of Professional Associations in Quality Assurance

Professional associations in Africa are also involved in higher education quality assurance. However, except for a few countries, their involvement is *ad hoc* and outside government authority. Their involvement comes in three forms: (1) accreditation of professional study programs in tertiary institutions (for example, Nigeria, South Africa); (2) participation in accreditation panels set up by national QA agencies (for example, Nigeria, Ghana, Tanzania); and (3) participation in curriculum review exercises (for example, Nigeria, Tanzania). A key strength of professional associations is that their legal mandates include licensing of graduates to practice after graduation. This serves as a deterrent that compels tertiary institutions to voluntarily open up their programs for professional accreditation, as failure to do so might deny their graduates the opportunity to be licensed as professionals.

With the exception of South Africa, the QA legal mandates of professional associations overlap with those of the respective national agencies. In South Africa, the mandate of the Higher Education Quality Committee (HEQC) as regards program accreditation does not include professional programs. In other countries, efforts to harmonize the two mandates have not always been successful because some associations are unwilling to cooperate, arguing that their mandate precedes the creation of the quality assurance agency. For example, in Nigeria at least ten professional bodies operate with a federal mandate to accredit professional training and set standards for members of the professions (including: engineering, chartered accountants, law, dentistry, medicine, ICT, nursing and midwifery). The NUC continues to accredit all programs, including professional programs that are also accredited separately by the professional associations (Jibril 2006). The positive side of this duplication is that even without public funding, quality assurance of professional programs is still assured since the associations cover their costs from member contributions.

One challenge associated with professional involvement in accreditation is the need to separate the advocacy or trade union function of the associations from its quality assurance functions. In the effort to achieve this by law, some countries (for example, South Africa) have created statutory professional bodies specifically for quality assurance.[30] Those bodies have their own standards, including required program structure and syllabi, which in some cases may not be the same as those of the national QA body. In Ghana, where a good relationship exists between the National Accreditation Board and a number of professional associations, the accrediting role of professional associations is very effective and relieves the government of the need to fund the process of accreditation for those programs. Nonetheless, there is a delicate balance between advocacy and quality review. It will be important for quality assurance agencies, ministries, and departments in those countries to put in place carefully considered rules on conflict of interest and mechanisms to insure transparency and maintain the legitimacy of the process.

Professional associations can also serve as an external check on the quality assurance processes of country's higher education system, especially in large systems where students can choose among many institutions offering similar programs. In Nigeria, for example, professional programs that fail accreditation by the respective professional association are deserted by students and employers because the professional accreditation process is perceived to be credible and transparent. Consequently, institutions whose programs fail usually take prompt action to rectify observed deficiencies. Perhaps in recognition of this fact, the NUC includes

30. The Health Professions Council of South Africa (HPCSA); The Council for the Regulation of Engineering Education in Nigeria (COREN) and the Council for Legal Education in Nigeria; and the Institute of Chartered Accountant in Ghana are good examples.

**Box 9: The Challenges of Cross-border Delivery of Higher Education in Tanzania**

The emerging challenges of cross-border delivery cannot be met by the Commission operating at the national level. Networking at regional and global levels is necessary. The regulations still envisage a campus university with halls of residence and *in situ* facilities for learning and teaching. New modes of delivery that are electronic do not require the type of infrastructure that is specified under the Act and its regulations.

*Source:* Mihyo (2006).

at least one representative of the relevant professional body in its accreditation panels and also holds biannual consultative meetings with these bodies. Considering the existing capacity constraints and the high costs of program accreditation, it would seem sensible to assign the responsibility for professional programs accreditation to respective associations while maintaining close cooperation between these associations, national QA agencies and HEIs.

## Quality Assurance in the Regional Context

The value of cross-border collaboration in quality assurance is increasingly being recognized globally and in Africa. The potential benefits of regional cooperation for quality assurance and accreditation are substantial. These encompass: mutual recognition of accredited status,[31] recognition of degrees,[32] mobility of students and faculty, cooperation providing peer reviewers and external examiners, and regional accreditation and quality assurance—an especially appealing prospect to small countries with only a few major universities.

The need for collaboration has become more urgent of late following the launching of WTO's General Agreement on Trade in Services (GATS) and recent advances in technology that have facilitated a rapid increase in cross-border provision of higher education. These developments have challenged the traditional approach to quality assurance because cross-border HE providers cannot easily be regulated by national QA agencies since with information technologies, they are capable of reaching the consumer (students) directly without the need for any authorization. Without cross-border collaboration in quality assurance, it is difficult, if not impossible to enforce accountability of providers to consumers. This opens the door to the risk of substandard education being delivered to unsuspecting students in developing countries, where the demand far exceeds the supply and where foreign credentials are perceived to be more valuable. Box 9 illustrates this challenge as regards cross-border provision of higher education in the case of the Higher Education Accreditation Commission in Tanzania.

---

31. Among the most successful regional agreements about recognition of accredited status is the Washington Accord (originally singed in 1989) by which signatory nations agree to recognize the accreditation status of the program accredited by each of the members of the accord. It includes: Australia, Canada, Hong Kong, Ireland, Japan, New Zealand, South Africa, United Kingdom, and the United States. For information on other international agreements see Hayward (2000).

32. See the Arusha Convention of 1980 on recognition of academic qualification. UNESCO is also working in this area. See its *Guidelines for Quality Provision in Cross-border Higher Education*, UNESCO, Paris, 2006.

At the global level, the International Network for Quality Assurance Agencies in Higher Education (INQAAHE) was established in 1991 with the purpose of collecting and disseminating information on current theory and developing practice in the assessment, improvement and maintenance of quality in higher education.[33] Within the European Union area, the Bologna process was launched in 1999 with the goal of strengthening European cooperation in quality assurance.[34]

More recently, with World Bank support, regional quality assurance networks have been established in the Asia-Pacific region (the Asia Pacific Quality Network—APQN) and in the Latin America and Caribbean region (RIACES). Within Africa, a number of subregional networks can be found whose mandates include collaboration in quality improvement in higher education. These are: the *Conseil Africain et Malgache pour l'Ensignement Supérieur* (CAMES), the Inter-University Council of East Africa (IUC-EA), the Southern African Development Community (SADC), the Southern African Regional Universities Association (SARUA), the Higher Education Quality Management Initiative for Southern Africa (HEQMISA), and the Association of African Universities (AAU). In addition, the North Africa and the Middle East region plans to establish an Arab Quality Assurance Network for Higher Education (ANQAHE) in which Egypt—one of the countries being assisted by the World Bank to set up a national QA agency—is playing a leading role.

## *Current Regional Initiatives*

The most developed regional initiatives in quality assurance in sub-Saharan Africa are based in CAMES, SADC, and the AAU. A brief description of these initiatives is given below.

*CAMES.* The *Conseil Africain et Malgasche pour l'Ensignement Supérieur* is an intergovernmental organization based in Ouagadougou, Burkina Faso. It was established in 1968 to promote equivalence of qualifications and awards, harmonize promotion of academic staff (evaluation of qualifications for promotion), and take responsibility for quality assurance in Francophone Africa. Since then, CAMES has also taken up responsibility for accreditation of new private HEIs in the region. Member countries and institutions are free to select which of the services offered by CAMES they would like to have. Anecdotal information indicates that not all countries request all CAMES programs.

With a current membership of 17 countries, CAMES is run by a small core team of two professional staff, 5 administrative staff and 4 supporting staff. This team is responsible for program accreditation of 400–500 programs every five years and an average of 43 institutional accreditations each year. Evaluation of programs and institutions is done through its various commissions. Impressively, secretariat staff (currently just two professionals) is

33. INQAAHE had 10 members when it was established in 1991. Currently it has over 100 members drawn from 55 countries. It's headquartered in Dublin Ireland (www.inqaahe.org).

34. The general objectives of the Bologna Process are the creation of a system of comparable degrees (diploma supplement), the creation of a three cycles degree system (undergraduate, graduate and PhD), the introduction of a credit point system (like ECTS), the promotion of mobility, the strengthening of European cooperation in quality assurance, and the promotion of a European dimension in higher education. Currently 44 countries are involved in the Bologna process.

responsible for managing the work of these commissions and verifying the accuracy and consistency of reports submitted by the commissions.

*The SADC Experience.*[35] The Southern African Development Community (SADC) was created with the signing of a Declaration and Treaty by Heads of State and Government at Windhoek, Namibia in August of 1992 to promote social, economic and political cooperation among its member states, now numbering fourteen.[36] The ultimate objective of the Community is to achieve a high degree of harmonization and rationalization that enables the pooling of resources to solve common problems.[37]

SADC countries differ significantly from one another with respect to the state of higher education. Tertiary education gross enrollment ratios ranges from 0.3 percent in Malawi to 12 percent in South Africa. The population range of SADC members is equally wide (about 1 million in Mauritius and Swaziland to 58 million in the Democratic Republic of Congo). Ideally, regional collaboration could be a powerful vehicle to achieve economies of scale since some of the countries are either too small or have too little capacity to sustain an effective QA system on their own.

Since the political transformation of South Africa in 1994, there has been an asymmetry in student mobility. Large numbers of students from other SADC countries study in South Africa, but few South Africans study in neighboring countries. In response, the SADC Heads of State signed *the SADC Protocol on Education and Training* which *inter alia* established a Technical Committee on Certification and Accreditation (TCCA) to develop policy guidelines and mechanisms to harmonize academic programs and qualifications in the region. But due to lack of funding, no progress has been registered. A parallel non-governmental initiative, the Higher Education Quality Management Initiative for Southern Africa (HEQMISA), was launched with donor support but has also not gained momentum due to similar constraints.

*The AAU Quality Assurance Initiative.* Established in 1962 and currently comprised of 194 member institutions from 45 countries, the Accra-based Association of African Universities (AAU) is uniquely positioned as an advocate for and convener of leaders, policymakers and development partners in higher education in Africa. Alarmed by declining quality of higher education, the AAU has since 1997 taken up quality assurance as a core theme of its strategic plan. This resolve has recently been reinforced by new global challenges to tertiary education emanating from cross-border higher education and GATS.

AAU's strategy is to work through a collaborative network comprising subregional higher education groupings, a global partnership of resource persons, and development partner organizations to build a critical mass of QA human capacity at institutional and national levels in each country. Through a partnership with the World Bank, the AAU intends to launch a new phase of its QA work in 2007 comprised of three program components:

35. This section on quality assurance regionally is a shortened version of the discussion in the case study report on South Africa by Daniel J. Ncayiyana (2006).

36. Member states of SADC are Angola, Botswana, Congo DRC, Lesotho, Madagascar, Malawi, Mauritius, Mozambique, Namibia, Tanzania, South Africa, Swaziland, Zambia, and Zimbabwe.

37. http://www.sadc.int/english/about/history/index.php?media=print (accessed March 18, 2006).

- Support for member universities of the AAU to develop strong internal quality assurance mechanisms. This will include training of self-evaluators and peer reviewers who would also be available to serve in accreditation/audit panels set up by national QA agencies.
- Support to existing and emerging Quality Assurance/Accreditation Agencies for development of capable external evaluation and monitoring systems within national higher education systems.
- Development and implementation of a Regional Framework on Recognition of Studies, Certificates, Diplomas, Degrees and other Academic Qualifications in Higher Education in Africa, based on the Arusha Convention,[38] as an instrument to enhance inter-university collaboration and student mobility.

### *Lessons from Existing Regional Initiatives in Africa*

The value of regional collaboration in higher education quality assurance and harmonization of programs and qualifications is well recognized in Africa. However, collaborative initiatives are constrained by several factors. Principle lessons learned from experiences to date are:

- Lack the core human capacity in their early stages. Consequently, their development is slow and unpredictable. As a result, the first step towards strengthening these initiatives has to entail building core capacity within the regional (or subregional) coordinating units themselves.
- Even with the strong political will of member countries, regional QA initiatives take a long time to develop and they can only be as strong as the institutions and national agencies in the member countries. For example, the SADC region QA initiative has benefited significantly from the experience of South Africa's quality assurance system and its higher education institutions. Strengthening the capacity of HEIs and national agencies in member countries is, therefore, a pre-requisite to the development of effective regional collaboration.
- Sustainable funding of regional QA initiatives is a major challenge in Africa. Most funding has so far come from international development partners. A likely explanation is the absence of political or civic pressure for governments to contribute to regional initiatives. This is an overarching problem with all regional bodies in Africa which is unlikely to be resolved soon given the weak economies of most countries.
- Support from donors remains the major source of funding for regional collaboration in quality assurance. Considering the potential benefits, long-term commitments from donors are needed to facilitate stability in planning and development. Unfortunately,

38. The Arusha Convention was launched by African ministers responsible for higher education in Africa in 1980 to promote cross-recognition of qualifications, programs and awards in Africa. For various reasons, on 15 countries have so far ratified it and given new developments since it was launched, major revisions are necessary.

such commitment has so far not been forthcoming. Multilateral financial institutions like the World Bank and the African Development Bank could play a key role in this regard through their convening power and their credit operations. Regional groupings could collectively, commit to large credits over an extended period to supplement local and bilateral donor sources. This is an area that requires greater attention by all parties, particularly as regards the further development of versatile instruments to facilitate easy access to such credits.

CHAPTER 4

# Cost Implications and Financing

Data on costs and financing of quality assurance are limited. In addition, costing of quality assurance processes is not easy, mainly because many hidden costs are involved. It is constrained by the absence of a common set of activities that constitute quality assurance, especially at the institutional level. Part of the problem is the magnitude of the task required to collect cost data and the difficulty of assigning costs to some activities. Some costs such as site visits (travel, lodging, meals) are clear cut. Similarly, the honoraria paid to peer reviewers are easily defined. The budgets of quality assurance agencies are also public information in most places so those costs can be identified. However, there are many subtle institutional costs, especially regarding preparation of self-studies, site visits, follow-up, and administrative preparation costs, that are very hard to calculate. Frequently these costs are hidden. For example, how does one factor in the time of university staff members who serve on the self-assessment committees? Is this part of their normal duties and thus has no cost? If that is the case, how does one factor in the opportunity costs which may result, for example, in a decrease in publications for those involved? What about administrative time? Is that also part of normal university operations? If a separate unit is established within an institution to oversee QA activities, should not the time it spends to supervise and prepare the self-study be added to the overall cost of accreditation or audits? These are not easy questions to answer and the study did not reveal clear cut responses. Nonetheless, some useful information was gathered from the case studies and this is presented in Table 6. The cost data are based on the various methods used by each country in recording QA costs.

**Table 6. Estimated Cost of Accreditation/Auditing Case Study Countries 2005/2006**

| 2005/2006 | Inst. Accreditation or Audit Visit Cost to National Agency | Program Accreditation Single Program (Average) | Total Cost to Run National Agency | Honoraria for Peer Reviewers | Charge to Institution for Accreditation or Audit | Cost to Inst. for Accreditation or Audit Self-Study & Visit | Who Pays Cost of Site Visit? |
|---|---|---|---|---|---|---|---|
| Cameroon | NA | NA | $200,000 | NA | None | | NCPHE |
| Ghana | $6,000 | $6,000 | $400,000 | $240 | Varies by size | | NAB |
| Nigeria | $3000–$5000 | $1,065 | $600,000 | $350 | Accommodation & board | | NUC |
| South Africa | NA | NA | $2,302,424 | NA | Fee varies | $25,000* | Institution |
| Tanzania | $5000–6000 | $4,000 | $580,000 | $300 | Fee charged | $20,000 | HEAC & Institution |

* Based on an estimate of one institution of the direct costs—i.e. not counting staff or faculty salary costs or time spent.

## Some Cost Estimates

### *Accreditation and External Audits*

Table 6 shows estimated costs for accreditation in the six case study countries. The estimated total annual cost for the national QA agency in five of the case study countries varied from US$200,000 in Cameroon to US$2.3 million in South Africa. The average cost of the four, excluding South Africa, is US$450,000 per year. Furthermore, based on the costs provided by three of the agencies for a single program review, the average cost is US$3,700 each. If a country has 150 programs to review and the same audit team does all of them at US$3,700 each (a very generous assumption), the total cost would be US$550,000.

The cost of institutional accreditation was estimated at about US$5,200 per visit. If there were fifteen institutions to be accredited or audited, the total cost would be US$78,000—much less than program accreditation. If a small number of program audits were added to that, ten for example, the total cost would rise to US$115,000.

The cost in human resources to sustain a fully-fledged and effective quality assurance system at the institutional and national levels is formidable. Program audits require four to five peer reviewers per program, with each reviewer involved in four or five programs over a period of time. Thus for an average country with about 150 programs, that would require at least that many reviewers. Can enough reviewers with distinguished reputations, high quality and good personal skills be found? Of the six case studies, only Nigeria was able to meet its peer reviewer needs without any reported difficulty. A related issue is the need to have competent professional staff at the national agency to review the various panel reports for consistency and completeness—a critical factor in ensuring the credibility and legitimacy of the results.

While external peer reviewers can be invited to augment limited country capacity, the cost per person ranges from US$3,000 to US$10,000 per visit, depending on the distance traveled and the length of the stay. On the other hand, the inclusion of foreign specialists, though costly, has advantages in providing expertise in areas where local expertise is limited and in helping to insure that where international benchmarks are important to the process, they are carefully assessed. An important lesson is that not every country can afford across-the-board program accreditation. Each country will have to make judgments about its own capacity, and adopt a phased introduction of QA processes that matches its state of development.

In addition to the direct costs to an institution being accredited or audited, substantial "hidden costs" are frequently present that are not always taken into consideration in the planning process. Key among these are pre-accreditation preparation costs and staff time before, during and after the accreditation/audit process. These costs are real. As the experience in several of the case studies demonstrates, they can pose real problems for the long-term viability of the process. Universities in both South Africa and Tanzania complained about the high costs of the process. In both cases, administrators felt they were too high to be sustainable in the long run. Two estimates were given—US$25,000 (South Africa) and US$20,000 (Tanzania)—not counting staff salary costs for time spent on the process. As the case of Nigeria illustrates (Table 7), when added to the other costs for the process, the cost per program can be substantially increased. In data from Rhodes University in South Africa, it was found that in the 18 month period it took to prepare the

**Table 7. Costs of Program Accreditation in Nigeria: 1999/2000–2005**

| Year | Number of Programs | Total cost (Naira)* | Estimated Total Cost (US$)** | Average Cost/Program (US$) |
|---|---|---|---|---|
| 1999/2000 | 1,198 | 998,539,000 | 7,132,421 | 5,953 |
| 2002*** | 182 | 324,774,400 | 2,319,817 | 12,746 |
| 2004*** | 42 | 93,340,400 | 666,717 | 15,879 |
| 2005 | 1,343 | 1,161,810,590 | 8,298,647 | 6,179 |

* Post-accreditation costs are excluded but amount includes pre-accreditation costs to institutions to prepare for accreditation.

** US$1.00 = approx. 140 Naira.

*** These are for maturing programs and newly established institutions and programs. Comprehensive program accreditation is carried out every 5 years.

self-study at Rhodes, some 450 staff, students, and faculty members were involved. That represents a very big investment in time—much of it away from their regular teaching, research and administrative duties. These realities need to be carefully taken into account at the planning stage.

Overall, it seems fair to assume that even a modest quality assurance effort in a country with ten tertiary institutions would cost at least US$700,000, that is, US$450,000 for the agency and at least US$250,000 for the institutions. That does not include the subsequent costs to institutions for changes needed to improve their chances of meeting standards (for example, upgrading science teaching labs, increasing the number of full time faculty, improving access to computers) and the time spent by staff on various aspects of the process.

A related cost that is critical to quality improvement is the post-accreditation expense to the system of addressing the observed weaknesses. Meeting these costs is absolutely important because it has direct effect on the fate of students already enrolled. The time available to address these shortcomings is therefore limited. In addition, if no help is provided to fix the shortcomings identified during accreditation/audit, there is less incentive to take QA preparation seriously. In Nigeria, for example, programs that are judged as partly deficient have up to two years to fix the observed deficiencies, otherwise they have to shut down the program. While not all of weaknesses have cost consequences, many of them do. However, no clarity exists as to who is responsible for covering these costs. Public HEIs claim that these costs ought to be covered by the governments that were responsible for the under-funding which led to poor quality in the first place. Governments, on the other hand, want HEIs to seek alternative sources of funding and/or undertake internal reforms to improve efficiency and thus free up funding to cover these costs. Both views have some merit, depending on the circumstances of each institution and country. In Ghana, getting government to respond to the obvious needs of the universities has been very difficult, though government support has improved slightly in the last year. In South Africa and Mauritius, the government has been more responsive, and the accreditation and audit processes have proven to be useful tools in leveraging the government and private support needed. In Nigeria, public institutions whose programs are identified as needing improvement are

**Table 8. Annual Costs of External Examiners at the University of Dar es Salaam, 2005/06**

*For 104 external examiners and about 350 courses*

| Cost Item | Cost [TShs] | Approx. Cost [US$]* |
|---|---|---|
| 1. Hotel costs | 75,900,000 | 54,873 |
| 2. Air tickets | 63,000,000 | 45,547 |
| 3. Honorarium | 77,000,000 | 55,668 |
| 4. Local transport, international calls, visa fees refund | 14,000,000 | 10,122 |
| **Total** | **229,900,000** | **US$166,210** |

Approx. (about US$475 per course; US$1600 per examiner, 3–4 courses per examiner) over one week

* Based on an exchange rate of US$1.00 = 1,383.19 Tanzanian Shillings as of 09/17/2006.

given priority for funding under the Education Tax Fund[39] if they submit convincing plans on how they intend to address the shortcomings. Though an assessment of the ETF impact on educational quality is possibly premature, availability of such a special funding facility is a powerful way to ensure the provision of resources needed to improve quality.

## *Cost of External Examiners*

No published data could be found on the costs and financing of external examiners in Africa. Even within institutions, such data are difficult to obtain since there is no culture of tracking and relating costs and financing to programs and learning outcomes. Limited data obtained from the University of Dar es Salaam in Tanzania show that even where external examiners are drawn from sister institutions within the same country or from neighboring countries, the cost per program can be almost 50 percent of the cost of program accreditation. As Table 8 indicates, the cost per program for the 2005/06 academic year was about US$475. The value-added of external examination is being questioned in many institutions. Examiners spend a maximum of one week with an average of three or four courses per examiner and, in some courses, several hundred students' scripts per course. In most cases, no mechanism is in place for the effective monitoring of the implementation of recommendations made by these examiners. It would seem more beneficial to utilize these external examination funds for institutional self-assessment supplemented by periodic external peer reviews or accreditation.

## *Cost of Regional Collaboration in Quality Assurance*

Little is currently known about the costs involved in regional collaboration in quality assurance. Available anecdotal information indicates that funding from local sources is

39. The Nigeria Education Trust Fund was established in 1993 with the objective of improving the quality of education in Nigeria. All corporations and companies of identified minimum operating capacity and registered in Nigeria contribute a levy of 2 percent of their annual assessable profits to the Fund which complements Federal, State and Local Government budgets for the three levels of education nationwide.

very limited. The CAMES annual budget of approximately CFA 580 million (about US$1.1million) is largely provided by its international development partners.[40] CFA 43 million comes from candidate institutions for accreditation which are charged CFA 1 million (about US$2,000) each and member governments contribute an additional CFA 10–20 million per year. Reliance on donor funding makes it difficult to ensure sustainability as there is no guarantee of continued funding after a particular grant is exhausted. Thus, although unlimited political will to pursue regional collaboration may be expressed, in reality regional collaboration is severely limited by uncertainty in funding.

## Financing of Quality Assurance

Budgets for national quality assurance agencies are public information, but they do not include data on financing of QA processes in tertiary education institutions. What is of concern, however, is the fact that there is currently no link between QA processes/results and public financing decisions for tertiary education. Without such a link, institutions lack the means and incentive to implement quality improvement recommendations. Similarly, governments miss an opportunity to influence accountability of public tertiary institutions.

In some countries, quality improvement funds have been set up, mainly with external support. Through a World Bank credit, Mozambique established a Quality Enhancement and Innovation Fund (QIF) in 2002, the implementation of which has been rated as "highly successful" (World Bank 2004b). Ethiopia recently established a similar facility—the Development Innovation Fund (DIF)—also through World Bank support to innovations in relevance, content, and quality of academic programs (World Bank 2004c). Ghana too has established a Teaching and Learning Innovation Fund (TALIF) with World Bank financing "to support improvement in quality, relevance and efficiency of the teaching and learning process." Similar funds are envisaged in Nigeria and Tanzania. While these funds are likely to have a positive impact on quality, their sustainability would be better assured if at the policy level a clear connection were made between the results of QA processes and financing decisions for institutions. Linking public financing (competitive funds and other public funding) to quality assurance processes and outcomes could play a key role in strengthening accountability and in encouraging institutions to undertake quality improvements.

40. Based on discussions with CAMES Management in Ouagadougou, June 2006.

CHAPTER 5

# Challenges and Opportunities

Compared to more developed higher education systems in the world, quality assurance systems in Africa are still at an infant stage and thus confronted by many challenges. Some of these challenges were highlighted in previous paragraphs. This section attempts to summarize the main capacity enhancement and knowledge development needs for African QA agencies, based on observations from the six detailed case studies. Table 9 summarizes the main constraints identified by country. These constraints and related issues are discussed in the following sections.

## Issues of Human Capacity

Effective quality assurance depends largely on the availability of highly qualified faculty members and administrators within institutions and competent professional and technical staff in national QA agencies. The success of accreditation, audits, and academic reviews is particularly demanding of human capacity since the legitimacy and credibility of the results is so dependent on the quality, dedication, and integrity of the people who serve as peer reviewers, the administrators and faculty members who prepare the self-assessment and collect needed data at institutions being reviewed, and the professional staff in the national QA agency who eventually review the panel reports and disseminate the results to stakeholders and the public. These individuals must not only be experts in their respective fields, but they must also be accepted as neutral parties to the process, and possess the personal skills and diplomacy necessary to conduct effective site visits. As illustrated in following paragraphs, QA systems in Africa (including those is countries with stronger economies like South Africa) are experiencing several constraints: the difficulty of finding a sufficient number of academics who are qualified and available to serve as peer reviewers; the lack of

**Table 9. Main Constraints to QA Development in Africa**

| | Cameroon | Ghana | Mauritius | Nigeria | South Africa | Tanzania |
|---|---|---|---|---|---|---|
| Insufficient human capacity | x | x | x | | x | x |
| Insufficient funding at agency and institutional levels | x | x | x | x | x | x |
| Lack of national QA policy | x | | | | | |
| Overlapping mandates with professional associations and with other tertiary QA bodies | x | x | | x | | x |
| Lack of QA standards for distance learning programs | x | x | x | x | x | x |
| Lack of appeals procedure for dissatisfied institutions | x | x | x | x | x | x |
| Insufficient communication within institutions about external QA processes | x | | | | | |
| Lack of incentives and sanctions to enforce compliance | x | x | x | | | x |
| Accreditation standards not linked to outcomes and skills needed by labor market | x | x | x | x | x | x |
| Lack of standards and mechanism to regulate quality of education from cross-border providers | x | x | x | | | x |

appropriate training for those involved in the process in the accrediting agencies, at institutions, and as peer reviewers; and problems for institutions to amass the data, information and self-analysis needed for effective self-studies.

## *Training for Staff of National QA Agencies*

Professional staff in national QA agencies requires two main types of skills sets—skills for system conceptualization and development of methodologies, and skills for implementation of QA processes. In the early stage of an agency' development (as is the case in most national agencies in Africa), the skills required have to do with capacity for analyzing the higher education context and conceptualizing appropriate QA systems, translating those into methodologies and procedures, and then understanding how and where to start the implementation. In most cases, senior staff appointed to lead such agencies initially knows little about QA, perhaps except for having been involved in research evaluations along with many years of teaching and research experience at universities. Thus, most of their QA learning takes place through reading materials and visiting other agencies with more experience.

The implementation phase requires an additional set of skills in order to ensure that the work is credible and has its own internal quality guarantees. The presence of senior staff with experience in higher education processes is critical. Often, as was the case in South Africa for example, teams includes younger staff who have never worked in a higher education institution and are unable therefore to bring those understandings to reports prepared by peer review panels. For these, training has two dimensions: first, to acquire an exposure to higher education processes and academic activities (including quality assurance) by attending conferences and also by spending some time in institutions of higher learning; and secondly, to obtain new knowledge, for example, through in-house writing workshops, seminars on QA topics and pursuit of graduate degrees in higher education). While the first does not require much funding, the second can be costly, especially because most countries do not have graduate programs in education that include a component on QA. The approach taken by South Africa of establishing memoranda of understanding (MoU) with other agencies for staff exchange visits is worth emulating for countries with young agencies. Active learning through regular internal reviews of the agency's work, diagnostic case studies of things that went wrong, and working through these cases as a learning exercise has also proved to be a reliable way of strengthening agency capacity.

One of the most critical problems faced in all of the cases except Nigeria was the scarcity of competent academics and professionals who could serve as peer reviewers. Even in South Africa, with a very large base of experienced faculty members and a sizeable pool of outstanding professionals, there was consensus that the magnitude of the audit and accreditation process was requiring far too much time from administrators and teaching staff. Added to the existing load of committee meetings and transformation forums in South Africa, the demands on staff is perceived to have contributed to a significant decline in publications over the last few years. Part of the problem could be attributed to the complexity of South Africa's QA system; however, these difficulties are largely a testimony to the huge staffing needs of accreditation if it is going to be done well and maintain its legitimacy.

Scarcity of peer reviewers is not a reflection of a lack of support by academics. A number of peer reviewers were interviewed during the study. All of them expressed their commitment to the process; indicated that the site visits were thoughtful, fair, and useful; and believed that accreditation and audits were making a significant contribution to improving educational quality. As one experienced peer reviewer put it in Ghana, "Without the accreditation process, the institutions in Ghana would be rotten." While this is no doubt overstating the case, the consensus in Ghana was that the QA process had halted the decline in quality of the 1980s and 1990s and fostered a marked improvement in quality in many areas.

Training of peer reviewers and pre-review preparations are in some cases insufficient. Most peer reviewers interviewed noted that the training they received was inadequate. They cited a number of examples of problems including: the training was too short with too little information about the process; there was no training at all—merely providing rating sheets and other practical information about the site visit; lack of information about the institution they were to review; failure to receive the institutional self-study prior to the visit; lack of clear guidelines about how to evaluate the standards and the institution in terms of the standards. In Ghana, for example, peer reviewers spoke of the lack of training

**Box 10. Comments by a Ghanaian Peer Reviewer on his Learning Experience as a Reviewer**

"They had a consolidation year for weaker students and an internship program in the final year for everyone. The students also did a minor in ICT while at the others institution they did only math. There was something beautiful happening at the second institution. The focus on teaching and on individual students was a real morale booster for the students. They were so happy, many of them found money to buy their own computers. The university had installed wireless for them. They created a real learning community with a commitment to teaching that helped raise standards. And watching them we learned things that will help us do the same thing in our own institutions."

Interview in Accra, Ghana, March 10–11, 2006

and the difficulty they had in getting basic information about the universities to be reviewed prior to their visits. One reported that the agency had sent him on a site visit with nothing but some questions to be answered. While these particular peer reviewers were distinguished seasoned faculty members and felt they were able to provide a good assessment of the institutions, they nonetheless were troubled by the lack of information and training.[41]

The use of peer reviewers is creating a positive learning effect and contributes to creating a "culture of quality" within the host institutions of the reviewers. Faculty members involved in accreditation and audit processes at other institutions get an in-depth exposure to other quality management systems—exposure which can contribute in positive ways to improving quality at their own institutions. Peer reviewers interviewed talked about the lessons they learned from site visits—lessons they felt were useful for improving quality at their own institutions. One of the peer reviewers reported, after reviewing math programs at two different universities, that he had learned a great deal from visits and had discovered a tremendous difference between the two programs. Both institutions had similar programs, roughly the same admission standards, and comparable budgets. But the results were very different with one much more successful than the other. The peer reviewer described the situation at the more successful university as shown in Box 10. He added that all students from the program with the ICT minor had obtained employment when they graduated in contrast to few of those from the other institution.

The use of external (foreign) peer reviewers offers potential benefits, but the costs involved should be carefully assessed before making a selection. In both Ghana and Mauritius, the accreditors intended to use a significant number of foreign peer reviewers to help insure quality standards and to give legitimacy to the process. As a member of the senior staff at the NAB in Ghana noted, "What we had in mind was to have someone from Europe or the USA on every panel, but the costs made that impossible and we have used only a few from South Africa and neighboring countries."[42] In Mauritius, where the budget of the Tertiary Education Commission is more robust, they have managed to have at least one foreign peer reviewer on each of their panels.[43] One approach to easing the high costs of

41. Interview in Accra, Ghana, March 10–11, 2006.
42. Interview in Accra, Ghana, March 10–11, 2006.
43. Interview, Mauritius, February 23, 2006.

foreign peer reviewers is to coordinate the visit such that a number of universities hold their reviews during the same time period and share the costs.

Institutional accreditation requires far less human resource capacity than program accreditation. Institutional accreditation/audit employs a limited number of peer reviewers, defined primarily by the number of institutions (one panel per institution) and the frequency of accreditation desired. Most countries can find the human resources needed for both the peer review and administrative requirements of institutional accreditation. Program accreditation, on the other hand, can create huge demands for staffing at the national agency and requires very large numbers of peer reviewers. In its 2005 system-wide accreditation exercise, Nigeria mobilized 500 professors to serve as peer reviewers for 1,343 programs in 48 universities and 5 colleges. It also places excessive demands on administrative and faculty time.

A more affordable strategy is to conduct institutional accreditation at regular intervals (say 5 years) and limit program accreditation to a small number of mostly professional programs, especially where accreditation is a necessary condition for licensing of graduates. As explained elsewhere in this report, professional associations already possess a tradition of program accreditation for their professions, the costs of which are borne by the associations themselves. However, implementation of this strategy requires close cooperation between existing professional associations (or groups of professionals) and national accreditation agencies so as to ensure harmonization of standards to meet both national and professional needs.

## Costs and Funding Constraints

Program accreditation is the most costly part of a quality assurance system. The broader the sweep, the more time needed for both the preparation of self-studies and for effective peer reviews of that material and of the institution during the site visit. A high quality self-study by an institution reduces the time needed for external peer review and thus lowers costs. Other main cost drivers are the number of standards or criteria to be reviewed, quality of data management by the institution, size and competence of peer review team, extent of support provided the peer review team, bureaucratic complexity of the review process, and the quality of the professional staff within the national QA agency who organize review visits and scrutinize review panel reports for adherence to set standards. Of the cases examined here, the approach of South Africa (which is often viewed by neighboring countries as the model to learn from) is clearly the most comprehensive, complex and the costly. As one of the members of the HEQC noted, "This is the Rolls Royce of quality assurance."[44] Countries seeking to develop national accreditation systems would be well advised to avoid simply copying a model that has been successful in another country. Instead, they would do better to adopt a phased development process that matches their resources availability. One possible option for this stepwise approach to limit the scope to institutional accreditation and work in collaboration with professional organizations in accreditation of critical professional programs.

44. Interview with HEQC, Pretoria, South Africa, March 9, 2006.

## Need for Effective Communication

The importance of consultations throughout the process of developing and implementing a quality assurance system is critical. Mauritius is a good example. Prior to the introduction of accreditation for private institutions, the institutions were given opportunities to provide feedback on the guidelines prepared by the Tertiary Education Commission (TEC). This feedback served as a useful resource in the revision of the TEC Act. In the end, private institutions were generally pleased with new the legislation and felt that accreditation of their programs by the TEC enhanced their legitimacy.[45] In South Africa the HEQC spent a great deal of time consulting with stakeholders during preparation of policies and standards and, as is the tradition in contemporary South Africa, took those consultations into consideration in preparing standards. Indeed, some critics of the HEQC argued that it spent too much time consulting. The director of the HEQC attached great importance to having an "upfront communications strategy" and was sensitive to concerns that while they had communicated well with the universities and technikons, they had not done particularly well in the public domain. HEQC is currently working to improve its public communication strategy.[46] The HEQC has also tried to enhance the effectiveness of site visits by conducting post-site visit surveys which have proven helpful in revising their policies and procedures. In several countries, pre-accreditation visits to institutions to explain the procedures and to give staff a chance to ask questions were reported to be very well received.

## Legitimacy of the Process

None of the quality assurance agencies reviewed suffers from a crisis of legitimacy. Nonetheless, this issue was close to the surface in several cases and voiced as a major concern by leaders of the accrediting agency, some peer reviewers, vice chancellors, faculty members, and other interested observers. It was most acute in relation to peer reviewers and the recognition that how they are perceived affects their legitimacy, and in the long run the acceptability and the utility of the process. The comments and concerns of some faculty members in the post-accreditation survey at Rhodes University in South Africa speak to the point. A small number of those surveyed had negative reactions to the peer reviewers, to what they felt was their lack of preparation, and to the amount of work involved for small benefits.[47] While these were minority views, they demonstrate the fragility of the legitimacy attached to the process and the damage that can be caused by peer reviewers who are not experts in their fields, who are unprepared for the site visit, or who are insensitive to the need to be impartial and respectful throughout review process.

The quality, integrity and professionalism of peer reviewers are other factors that can compromise the legitimacy of the QA process. Comments from peer reviewers who felt they were neither sufficiently trained nor provided with ample information prior to site

---

45. Interviews with a number of leaders of private higher education institutions in Mauritius, Feb 17–21, 2006.

46. Interview with the Executive Director, HEQC, March 9, 2006.

47. For more details see Ncayiyana (2006), p. 17.

visits, suggest additional problems that can interfere with the effectiveness of the review. The case of the former quality assurance agency—*Agence Nationale d'Evaluation* (AGENATE)[48]—in Madagascar which failed because it lacked legitimacy suggests that once legitimacy is lost, it is almost impossible to regain it. Thus the training selection and training of peer reviewers, their preparation for site visits, and their deportment and integrity during and after the site visit are vital to the legitimacy and long term success of the process.

## Autonomy for Quality Assurance Agencies

A QA agency is responsible for assuring its own quality as there is normally no other oversight body responsible for this function. The legitimacy of the QA processes by national agencies, therefore, depend in large part on keeping the process transparent, open, and free of political and special-interest influences. While this is not currently an issue, as the process matures and more private institutions come on board, it may become more contentious as private institutions might demand that the system be free from government influence and/or political influence that might favor public institutions. In Egypt, for example, the QA agency started out as a government parastatal but it has now evolved into an almost fully autonomous body with broad independence from government. At the present time, three of the six quality assurance agencies examined in the case studies regard themselves as semi-autonomous (Ghana, Mauritius, South Africa). One way to increase the independence of QA agencies is to insist on greater institutional participation in covering the cost of accreditation (as South Africa, Nigeria and CAMES do to some extent). Complete autonomy might not be possible nor even necessary. In the long run, however, it will be important to develop policies and mechanisms that ensure the transparency and independence of the QA process and protect it from special interests of any kind in order to protect its legitimacy.

## QA for Distance Learning and E-learning

Almost all of the quality assurance agencies operating in Africa are given responsibilities over distance and e-learning programs. On the whole, however, very little quality assurance work has been done on either distance education or e-learning in the region. In some cases, the quality assurance process is just beginning, as in Tanzania, where the Open University of Tanzania is preparing to undergo its first accreditation. South Africa has a relatively long experience with distance learning institutions, particularly the University of South Africa (UNISA) and Technikon South Africa, which have large student bodies and years of operation. However, since the country's current accreditation and audit processes are very new, there is little experience with national quality assurance in this area.

This is a challenge that has posed problems for accreditors in other parts of the world as well (CHEA 2002). In response, guidelines, standards and policies have been developed for this purpose. The UNESCO/OECD Guidelines on *Quality Provision in Cross-border Higher*

48. The case of AGENATE in Madagascar prior to this study.

*Education* provide a valuable reference for developing national guidelines.[49] International cooperation with other accrediting agencies can also provide opportunities to learn from their experiences and develop standards and guidelines to forestall problems in this difficult but growing area of tertiary education.

## Tension between Public and Private Institutions

Until recently, public higher education institutions in most of Africa have resisted national accreditation efforts on the grounds that they are accredited *de jure* by the government charters or acts that created them. The Ghana government, after a long and divisive debate and strong resistance by public institutions, resolved the question by issuing a directive that all tertiary institutions, public and private, would be subject to accreditation within six months of the Act (2002). In Tanzania public higher education institutions were included in the accreditation process only beginning in 2005. The issue continues to be hotly debated in Madagascar where the public institutions assert that because they are statutory bodies created by Parliament, they should not be subject to accreditation. On the other hand, public institutions have been among the strongest advocates of accreditation for private tertiary institutions (for example, Kenya, Ghana, and Mauritius). Proponents have argued that the public must be protected from excessive entrepreneurialism, and that accreditation of private tertiary institutions is an appropriate mechanism to set minimal standards and guarantee quality to safeguard the public interest. These arguments seem disingenuous in the context of declining quality and the lack of coherent quality assessment at most public institutions. Indeed, private tertiary institutions feel unfairly treated and often believe that the public universities are using accreditation to limit competition from private institutions. Though this tension appears to have been resolved at the legal level through recent changes in legislation, it needs to be closely monitored in order to encourage increased private participation in higher education to supplement limited government capacity and to ensure accountability of public HEIs to tax-payers.

## Placing the Responsibility for Quality on the Institutions

Though it is generally agreed that the primary responsibility for quality assurance and improvement rests with the individual HEIs, the establishment of QA agencies in some African countries has been perceived (particularly by QA agencies themselves) as transferring the responsibility for quality assurance to an external body. As indicated in Box 11, overreliance on compliance to regulations imposed by an external body can work against quality improvement in HEIs (Hall 2005). In some cases, this has led to poor cooperation between institutions and the national agency particularly in countries that have implemented

49. The UNESCO/OECD *Guidelines on Quality Provision in Cross-border Higher Education* were issued in October 2005 following the UNESCO General Conference. The Guidelines are an educational response to the growing commercialization of higher education based on United Nations and UNESCO principles. Accessible at: http://portal.unesco.org/education/en/ev.php-URL_ID=41508&URL_DO=DO_TOPIC&URL_SECTION=201.html

**Box 11: Risk of Overreliance on Externally Imposed Regulations**

One strong theme that emerges from international experience is that quality assurance systems that overly rely on compliance to externally-imposed regulation may work against the interest of quality development in universities. This is partly because academics are intrinsically motivated, accustomed to autonomy and oriented towards a tradition of collegial peer evaluation. It is also because of the drain that compliance systems place on participating institutions; it has been argued that these sorts of quality assurance regimes require an unacceptable sacrifice of time by academic staff who would otherwise be conducting the primary functions of teaching and research.

*Source:* Hall (2005).

program accreditation. That is quite in contrast to the history of accreditation in the United States for example, which began with institutions seeking external feedback on the quality of their academic programs and inviting external peers to visit and report on what they saw. On the other hand, the crisis of quality in African higher education cannot be solved by the institutions themselves. Many would agree that some kind of external pressure is needed to foster quality improvement. However, it is also true that part of the blame for the decline in quality in HEIs in Africa can be attributed to governments for having insisted on expanded access at the same time that they were cutting funding, keeping a strong hold on governance, the choice of vice chancellors, the hiring of staff, and the freedoms and autonomy that are regarded as essential to creativity and learning in higher education.

Is it possible to implement a voluntary quality assurance system that leads to improved quality? South Africa is experimenting with the idea of self-re-accreditation and self-audits for institutions that have done well on previous reviews and meet certain requirements. In part, this is a response to pressures to reduce the complexity and the scope of accreditation. In other countries, discussions are taking place about limiting the extent of program accreditation to lessen the load on universities which would otherwise have to entertain quality reviews for all of their programs. These are complex issues, but it is encouraging to see discussion underway about appropriate mechanisms to guarantee and foster quality without imposing undue and counterproductive burdens. In the end, the responsibility for quality assurance and improvement rests squarely with tertiary institutions and their faculty members. The challenge is to make this happen while exercising great care to protect both institutional autonomy and the legitimacy and integrity of the quality assurance processes.

## Accountability and Link to Labor Market Needs

External accreditation and audits by national agencies appear to be playing a role in fostering greater accountability by tertiary institutions. Preliminary findings suggest that QA processes have helped engender a new sense of concern about improving teaching, learning, research, and public service in many higher education institutions. In a few cases, accreditation and audit processes have reversed or slowed the downward spiral in the quality of higher education, with Nigeria and South Africa being prime examples, and begun to move institutions and systems in the direction of global competitiveness. Both Nigeria and South Africa have a criterion related to employability of graduates in their accreditation scoring frameworks. Anecdotal information from the Nigeria and South Africa case studies suggest that employers, parents and prospective students are beginning to pay attention to the results of accreditation processes. A detailed assessment of this effect is beyond the scope of this study and may be premature. At a later date, it would be useful to conduct a follow-up study to assess more fully the impact of QA processes on relevance of outputs to the labor market, institutional accountability to funding bodies, and government accountability (and private funding sources) to institutions and the public.

### *What Are the Options to Address These Challenges?*

Weak human capacity, limited funding, and lack of convincing evidence of the direct impact of QA on educational quality and relevance of graduates are the main current constraints to development of QA in Africa. However, evidence from other countries shows that options exist for a nation to take a phased approach to developing a QA system. The following sections present some promising practices and discuss possible options for consideration with specific recommendations for QA agencies, tertiary institutions, and international development partners.

CHAPTER 6

# Innovations and Promising Practices

The quality assurance processes reviewed in this study provided evidence of several interesting innovations and practices that may be worth emulating by institutions and countries intending to set up or enhance their quality assurance systems.

## Pilot Quality Audits and Accreditation Reviews

South Africa and Egypt made extensive use of pilot audits and pilot accreditation reviews during the development phase of their accreditation and audit processes. Those proved to be very helpful in pointing out procedures that were cumbersome or needed clarification, identifying standards and criteria that were too complicated or lacked utility, and helping the agency to simplify a process that had become overly complex. It also proved beneficial to the institutions in giving them a dry run in the process, early feedback on quality and quality assurance procedures, and experience they could share with other institutions.[50] Such pilot assessments are highly recommended for all new accreditation and audit programs.

## Institutional Quality Assurance Committees/Units

Several accrediting agencies encourage the establishment of a quality assurance committee or unit at each higher education institution.[51] This provides a central focus and contact

50. This process is elaborated further in the South Africa case study by Daniel Ncayiyana (2006).

51. In Pakistan such a project started as a pilot program with start-up funding for each institution for a quality assurance cell to be headed by someone at the level of dean.

point for institutional accreditation and audits, program accreditation, and academic reviews. It also creates a base of information and institutional memory from one accreditation or audit review to the next (especially important where there are multiple program accreditation reviews), facilitates staff and peer review training, coordinates implementation of recommended quality improvement measures, and can help foster a *culture of quality* on campus. With that in mind, among the first steps taken in Sudan in establishing the accreditation process was to encourage and assist in the establishment of quality evaluation units in thirty-eight tertiary education institutions.[52] Establishment of such units is recommended for all HEIs, even in the absence of a national QA agency.

## Institutional Mentoring for Higher Education Institutions

Two of the case study countries have developed mentoring systems for new universities, or for private universities, not unlike those employed in an earlier era for some of the first universities in Africa. In Cameroon, the government has a mandatory system of mentoring in which private higher education institutions choose a mentor from among the public institutions and sign a mentorship agreement with the state and/or the accredited university as part of the conditions for accreditation. The costs of this relationship are borne by the private institution being mentored. In these cases, the degree granted during the mentoring period is that of the public university. Ghana has a somewhat similar process for its private universities. This arrangement is not without its critics, especially given the fees charged and proposed by the mentoring institution—recently set at US$17,000 by the University of Ghana. Private universities do have the option, after four years, if they fulfill certain conditions, to become universities in their own right and dispense with mentorship (Saffu 2006). One private Ghanaian university is in the process of seeking full university status at the present time.

## Encouraging Academic Reviews Independent of Accreditation

Most of the case study countries have some universities that have carried out independent institutional academic self-assessments. Several excellent examples of institutional academic reviews independent of the quality assurance process at national level are described in the case study reports on Tanzania, Ghana, and South Africa. What they suggest is the powerful advantages accruing to those institutions that do them. These institutions take on the burden of regular quality assessment, identify weaknesses on their campuses prior to any external review, and thus have the opportunity to quietly rectify problems and deficiencies identified. The case of the Kwame Nkrumah University of Science and Technology in Kumasi, Ghana is an excellent example. The ongoing efforts of its vice-chancellor and its Quality Assurance Unit helped transform the university and raise quality levels at a time when standards were generally falling in Ghana. Similar examples are noted in the case studies on South Africa and Tanzania (University of Dar es Salaam).

52. Interview with the director of the Evaluation and Accreditation Corporation (EVAC), Nairobi, Kenya, February 8, 2006.

The success of these autonomous institutional academic audits suggests that quality assurance agencies should encourage higher education institutions to undertake academic reviews on their own, outside the accreditation process. This is an excellent way to foster a *culture of quality* and to help institutions upgrade their faculties, departments, and programs without the public embarrassment of mediocre accreditation results. Support could be in the form of workshops to demonstrate the methods and utility of such academic program self-assessment, funding to assist HEIs in starting academic reviews or to help them with start-up costs of setting up Quality Assurance Units at their institutions.

## Financial Support for Quality Improvement

Among its various purposes, Nigeria's Education Tax Fund provides financial support to HEIs to improve quality, especially when quality improvement measures are recommended during accreditation. This is an encouraging example of a home grown solution to quality problems. By applying a competitive but formative approach to access such funds, institutions are tasked to ensure that funds so provided are used for priority needs. Other countries could consider developing similar approaches where they do not already exist. Availability of such funding encourages institutions to undertake quality improvement and also increases the relevance of the accreditation process.

The use of competitive quality improvement funds (QIF, DIF, and TALIF) as established by Mozambique, Ethiopia ad Ghana through their cooperative programs with international development partners (in this case the World Bank) is another effective way to not only strengthen quality but also to catalyze needed reform and innovation. It is necessary, however, to ensure that eventually these funds are backed by an appropriate funding policy and practice so that they may be sustainable beyond the life time of the respective donor-funded projects.

CHAPTER 7

# Options for Capacity Enhancement

## Recommended Options for National Agencies and HE Institutions

### *Setup and Implementation of QA Systems*

Systematic quality assurance processes are now in place within about one-third of African countries. In addition, efforts to establish QA systems are underway in several other countries (for example, DRC) as well as efforts to set up regional and subregional networks to facilitate sharing of experiences and expertise in QA. Although the QA processes being implemented vary substantially, most include self-studies by institutions, utilize peer reviewers, carry out site visits (mostly to private institutions), and produce a written report and recommendations for the public record. Only Mauritius, Nigeria, and South Africa have conducted accreditation of programs in public higher education institutions. The trend is likely to grow as Ghana, Uganda, and Tanzania have recently amended their laws to empower their national agencies to accredit programs in public institutions.

From the experience of the agencies reviewed (Cameroon, Ghana, Mauritius, Nigeria, South Africa, Tanzania), two general observations emerge. First, all existing national agencies are very young. None has been in existence for more than 15 years and most were set up in the last ten years. Second, depending on the approach taken, one may encounter significant differences in cost, human capacity requirements, time needed to participate effectively in the process, startup time, and training required. Program accreditation is the most costly and time-consuming. The main constraints are found in their human capacity requirements and their cost. Some of the approaches, such as those applied in South Africa, Mauritius, and Nigeria, are probably beyond the financial and human capacity of most African countries at their present levels of development.

For those contemplating quality assurance programs, what guidance can be offered by these case studies? What kinds of choices should those thinking about national quality assurance consider? Should the focus be on accreditation? Audits? Academic review? Some or all of them? A range of options is available for consideration by countries contemplating the establishment of national quality assurance systems. The main categories are:

- Institutional self-reviews/audits only,
- Institutional accreditation only (Ethiopia, Kenya, Madagascar),
- Institutional accreditation and accreditation of all programs for private universities (Cameroon),
- Institutional accreditation and accreditation of all programs for all universities (Tanzania, Uganda),
- Institutional accreditation and limited program accreditation (Ghana),
- Institutional audits and accreditation of all programs (South Africa and Mauritius),
- Accreditation of all programs only (Nigeria), and
- Ranking (Nigeria as part of program accreditation).

The challenge is how to achieve a healthy balance among the desire to excel in accordance with international standards, the mandate to respond to national needs and expectations, and the constraints in resources that remain a perennial problem.

Perhaps the most critical choice is whether or not to undertake both institutional and program accreditation, and if the latter, the breadth of program accreditation. The amount of funding likely to be available for the process should also affect choices. Where funding is restricted, the most appropriate strategy is to limit activity to institutional self-audits (though this might have less international appeal) followed by institutional accreditation, if funding permits. If program accreditation is carried out, it should be limited to critical professions such as health, engineering, and agriculture to start with, much as currently done by CAMES.[53] The number of programs assessed can be expanded at a later date if funding and human capacity allow.

It should be noted that accreditation criteria in the developed countries are in the process of moving from technique specifications to outcomes assessment (i.e., competency-based assessment). As this trend is expected to continue, quality assurance agencies in Africa are advised to consider outcomes assessment as their preferred approach. Indeed tertiary technical education in Ghana is already headed in that direction.

## Capacity to Implement QA Processes

*One of the lessons from the case studies is the importance of understanding the human capacity requirements of the accreditation and audit processes before putting the system in place.* The limited availability of the human capacity needed for effective quality assurance is among the most vexing problems facing quality assurance in Africa. It is a serious constraint in every case except Nigeria. Even in countries with large scale, mature, higher education systems

53. In work done by the World Bank in Pakistan for the Policy Note in 2005 and 2006, 165 programs in higher education were identified.

like that of South Africa, the human capacity demands have put the system under severe strains even at this early stage of implementation.

Where human resource shortfalls exist, agencies can either: (i) use expertise from other countries if funding is available; or (ii) adopt a more limited strategy. Lessons from case study countries point to the need for continuous training of peer reviewers in institutions of higher learning and agency staff. Professional staff leading QA processes have to be of a high quality since the integrity, credibility and legitimacy of the work done by the agencies depends on this. Frequent changes in direction or in the quality of assessment processes could be detrimental to the integrity and legitimacy of the process and the use of unqualified people as peer reviewers and as administrators of quality assurance agencies could be fatal to the process.

Adequate management capacity at the institutional and national agency levels are key to the quality of work done at these levels. Within institutions, experience from the case studies strongly suggests the need for a dedicated quality assurance unit within each institution to be responsible for overseeing implementation of quality improvement activities, and to ensure continuous monitoring and evaluation. At the agency level, professional and technical staff must have the requisite knowledge, skills and integrity.

Training of QA agency staff should be a continuous process. While academic backgrounds are necessary, QA agency staff require additional skills training—skills for system conceptualization and development of methodologies, and skills for implementation of QA processes. *There is currently no formal training available in this area.* For staff possessing little experience with higher education QA systems, training should focus on providing exposure to higher education QA processes. Such training can be obtained through attending conferences, spending some time in institutions of higher learning, study visits to other QA agencies, and in-house writing workshops and seminars on QA topics. Establishing memoranda of understanding (MoU) with other QA agencies for staff exchange and training purposes is a worthwhile strategy for countries with young agencies. Experience also shows that active learning through regular in-house reviews of the agency's work is a powerful and cost-effective way to strengthen agency staff capacity and to build team spirit.

### *Costs of Accreditation and Audits*

The broader the sweep, the more time required for the preparation of self-studies and for effective peer reviews of those prepared materials and the institution itself during the site visit. While the quality of the self-study will effect the time needed for a review to some extent, the major factors involved will be the number of standards or criteria to be reviewed, data requirements of the university, the expected depth of that review, and the complexity of the assessment process. Of the cases examined here, South Africa's methodology was clearly the most complex and the most costly. New entrants to the QA process would be well advised to limit initially the scope of their efforts to institutional accreditation and critical professional programs.

### *Capacity-building Needs*

The most critical need for establishing effective quality assurance systems identified during the study was practical training. Specifically, training is required for staff of national agencies, professional organizations, university senior staff, quality assurance unit staff, and peer reviewers. The challenge is how to develop a pool of QA human capacity in Africa at affordable cost and in a manner that can be sustained over time. Ultimately, any capacity-building initiatives taken have to be tailored to the African context (weak and fragile economies, varying sizes of tertiary education systems, limited and overstretched human capacity).

Subregional, regional and international partnerships seem to have a potential for accelerating the development of HE quality assurance in Africa, especially in small countries or post-conflict situations. These groupings provide opportunities for QA staff to learn from each other and to share resources—thereby leveraging economies of scale. Partnerships could also serve as a training ground for peer reviewers and QA agency staff. Contacts made in such sharing forums often last long after the events themselves are over and allow people with similar responsibilities to exchange ideas, experiences, and suggestions over an extended period.

### *HEIs Bear Primary Responsibility for Quality*

The primary focus of national QA agencies and institutional management should be to encourage HEIs to adopt a culture of quality in all their activities, taking into account national needs and global trends. This is particularly true in SSA where HEI are, in most countries, the only places with a concentration of highly trained staff with the qualifications to lead quality development in the country and serve as the primary source of peer reviewers for national QA agencies. Capacity-building efforts should therefore concentrate on building and retaining the institutional capacity to manage quality.

An effective communication strategy to educate students, parents, employers and the general public on the activities of a national QA agency or institutional quality assurance unit is necessary for maintaining the credibility of QA processes. Communication strategies have borne fruit with all the accreditors reviewed in this study. South Africa has been particularly resourceful in using the Internet, newspapers, radio and television. If accreditation and audits are to be effective, the public must understand the process and know how to access information about accredited/audited institutions in order to make educational decisions and be protected from fraud.

HEIs need to plan for the considerable institutional cost associated with accreditation—costs of site visits, self-assessments, and program reviews. The more extensive the demands of the self-assessment and site visit, the higher the costs. Two estimates of institutional costs obtained from the case studies were $20,000 and $25,000 without figuring staff time or salaries. Institutional requirements, self-study expectations, and site visit policies need to be carefully thought through to insure that the time and money invested will result in a comparable quality assurance finding and enhance the process of quality improvement.

## Possible Role for Development Partners

### *Share Knowledge and Expertise Accumulated from Projects in Other Regions*

The World Bank has been involved in several projects in recent years that have had quality assurance and accreditation as integral parts of its investments. These include projects in

Bangladesh, Cameroon, Chile, Egypt, Ethiopia, Ghana, Madagascar, Mozambique, Pakistan, Romania, and The Gambia. The Bank's experience accumulated over the years, coupled with its financial assistance program to countries, is an invaluable resource that could be tapped to strengthen the quality of higher education in Africa.

### *Support Establishment of Capacity-building in National QA Agencies*

For countries with large tertiary education systems, Bank-funded project support could be directed to the establishment of national QA bodies, the training of a critical mass of peer reviewers within agencies as well as within institutions, and the setting up of QA systems within individual tertiary institutions. Assistance could also be provided to support peer-to-peer learning among those involved in quality assurance within Africa and between African QA agencies and those in other regions (for example, Latin America, Eastern Europe, the United States, India and China) where QA systems are more mature.

### *Establish Competitive Quality Improvement Funds Through Education Projects*

The emerging trend by governments to establish competitive quality improvement funds deserves encouragement by international development partners as these funds serve as an incentive for institutions to improve quality and to participate in external reviews of their programs. Planning for the establishment of these funds should be accompanied by realistic plans for sustainability beyond the project duration in order not to create unmanageable expectations.

### *Encourage Regional Collaboration, Particularly for Small Countries, to Devise Capacity-Sharing Approaches to Quality Assurance, Including Cross-Border HE Quality Issues*

The World Bank and other development partners could also leverage their convening power to encourage and support regional collaboration in higher education quality assurance. This is particularly important for small countries, most of which have very young tertiary education systems. Through regional collaboration, smaller countries could get assistance from larger, more developed ones rather than establishing and maintaining their own QA agencies. Cooperation could take the form of sharing technical expertise, knowledge, and solutions in support of cost-efficient QA reviews. Collaboration could also devise solutions to cross-border HE quality issues (for example, developing standards for accreditation of open and distance learning programs, better understanding on the impact of GATS, brain drain, mechanism for cross-border recognition of programs, awards and certificates, etc.).

### *Monitor and Nurture the Development of Quality Assurance in the Region*

The Bank could also play the role of a global observatory of QA developments. In this context, the Bank would systematically monitor and review global QA developments and provide advice and documentation to countries on a range of important QA topics. Access to materials on QA, opportunities for staff training, and access to technical specialists in accreditation and quality assurance were the most frequently mentioned needs during site visits. Assistance could include new approaches to assuring quality, information on opportunities for QA capacity-building, innovative experiences from other QA bodies worldwide, materials on the development of standards for accreditation, self-study manuals from different regions, ethical issues in accreditation and ranking, etc.

### *Encourage and Fund Institutional Academic Reviews*

The value of individual academic reviews in African universities and other tertiary institutions resides in creating a *culture of quality* by putting the onus for quality assurance in the hands of individual universities, their faculty members and administrators. Academic reviews allow institutions to assess their own programs, identify weaknesses and needs, and work to improve quality on their own. They help institutions identify problems and seek solutions that will increase their success. The World Bank, through its engagement programs with countries (possibly supported under the newly introduced Africa Catalytic Fund), could encourage the development of a culture of quality within institutions of higher learning through various capacity-building activities.[54] This could include workshops on methods and procedures for academic reviews, the provision of start-up funding, and technical assistance with regard to self-studies, internal (or external) peer reviews for the programs examined, report preparation, and remedial funding to enable institutions correct quality deficiencies identified in the course of individual academic program reviews. Such programs would lay the groundwork for quality assurance in places where it is not yet in place, and reinforce an emerging *culture of quality* where QA is already practiced.

## Knowledge Gaps

### *Cost and Financing*

Information on cost and financing of higher education quality assurance processes is very limited. In particular, poor understanding surrounds the link between financing of higher education and the quality of outputs (graduates and research outputs). Within institutions, quality improvement financing and costs are usually lumped with other academic activities. Further work in this area is needed as part of the process of grounding the need for additional investments in quality improvement. Such a study might best focus on specific country case studies, particularly those which have had a relatively long history with formal QA processes like Nigeria.

### *Key Performance Indicators*

Currently very little is available in terms of performance indicators for assessing the effectiveness of QA processes at the institutional and system level in relation to their responsiveness to social demand and the needs of the labor market. Without such indicators,

54. A similar program was carried out in South Africa from 1993 to 1997 by the American Council on Education with 15 historically disadvantaged universities and technikons, assisted by Ford Foundation and USAID funding.

governments, tax-payers and the public lack an objective mechanism for assessing the impact of investments in quality assurance systems, and applicants to HEIs lack verifiable information to help them decide on the quality and relevance of education offerings at their prospective institutions.

### *Quality Assurance in Non-university Tertiary Institutions*

The number of non-degree granting tertiary institutions in Africa is large, diverse and growing. These institutions play a critical role in the production of medium and highly skilled human resources. Yet, little is known about how quality assurance should function in these institutions. In some countries, these institutions are being converted to universities. There are unanswered questions as regards the specific niches that these institutions serve, whether the types of programs they offer actually target these niches, and whether they have a distinct future. These and other questions need to be addressed with some urgency. To start with, a mapping exercise to establish a typology of these institutions would be useful.

### *How Can Accreditation Systems in Africa Measure the Quality of University Graduates Against Global Standards?*

Progress towards agreement on global standards for the licensing of graduates is occurring in certain professional fields, for example, the Washington Accord standards for engineering. This movement is likely to become more pervasive in the years ahead. Graduate competence that can be assessed in terms of global standards is important for companies considering foreign direct investment, and for graduates seeking mobility in a global labor market. Consequently, national licensing and accreditation norms that measure up to global standards, or at least can be calibrated against them, will likely need to be developed over time within Africa.

### *The Bologna Process and Its Impact on Higher Education in Africa*

Due to historical reasons, many African countries have strong links to European HEIs that are involved in the Bologna Process. The LMD degree structure, which was developed for the purpose of harmonizing academic programs across the European Higher Education Area, has now been adopted by the majority of French-speaking countries in Africa. For many of the African countries that have chosen to adopt this system, it is seen as an opportunity to introduce reforms in higher education—reforms that are indeed desirable. However, there are concerns as to how best to adapt the LMD system to the African environment, what might be its implications for quality assurance, and what might be the impact of consequent student and skilled labor mobility on African economies. In addition, African academics, particularly those in English-speaking countries, do not fully understand the Bologna process and its influence on global higher education. A study on the specific implications of the Bologna reforms for African higher education is therefore recommended.

APPENDIX

# Summary Status of HE Quality Assurance Implementation in Africa

## Methodology

A standard template was used to collect information on quality assurance for the 52 countries in Africa. Desk review of published information and online research from respective Ministry of Education websites and those of other institutions concerned with higher education in Africa provided the bulk of the information. In addition, telephone interviews were held with education or cultural attachés of some embassies based in Washington, DC where limited or no data could be found in the public domain. Once the templates were filled in, the responsible authorities in each country were requested (by electronic mail or via fax) to verify the data entered and/or provide additional data. But despite numerous efforts to follow up, only 14 countries reviewed the templates and sent back their responses. These countries were Cameroon, DRC, Ethiopia, The Gambia, Ghana, Madagascar, Mauritius, Nigeria, Seychelles, South Africa, Sudan, Tanzania, and Uganda.

## Limitations

Most ministries of education and some accreditation agencies lacked dedicated websites with comprehensive, up-to-date and historical information. One had to surf different websites to gather the information, which was time-consuming and frequently the results obtained were out-dated. For example, a very helpful website, INHEA, was last updated in 2000 and though it offered useful information, much of it was possibly outdated. Some websites were dysfunctional at the time the research was conducted. Embassy personnel contacted did not seem to have sufficient information about the responsibilities that their governments have toward quality assurance. In most cases, they referred our questions to their ministries of education.

## Findings

### *Countries with National QA Agencies*

Out of 52 countries, only 16 (31 percent) have quality assurance agencies. These are: Cameroon, Cote D'Ivoire, Egypt, Ethiopia, Gabon, Ghana, Kenya, Liberia, Libya, Mauritius, Mozambique, Namibia, Nigeria, South Africa, Sudan, Tanzania, Tunisia, Uganda, and Zimbabwe. Except for the six case study countries, the researchers had difficulty finding sufficient information in the public domain on the extent to which these agencies are implementing quality assurance processes. Table A.1 lists the countries with established national QA agencies. The number of HEIs in the country is also given in order to provide a sense of the size of the higher education system in the country.

### *Countries Without a QA Agency*

Some 36 countries (69 percent) have no national quality assurance agencies in place. These countries are listed in Table A.2. Some Ministries of Education have established dedicated units for quality assurance (operating as a directorate/department of the ministry) but no information was available on how they conduct business, or on the effectiveness of these structures in enforcing and maintaining standards. The table indicates whether or not the respective country has responded to confirm information on the template.

Table A.1. Countries with Legally Established National QA Agencies

| | Country | QA Authority | Year Created | Level of Autonomy* | Public HEIs | Private HEIs | Mandate of QA Agency |
|---|---|---|---|---|---|---|---|
| 1 | Cameroon | Council of Higher Education & Scientific Research (CHESR) | 1991 | No | 6 | 18 | CHESR accredits private institutions only. As of Sept 2003, a total of 11 institutions had received authorization to open; 7 had interim authorization and 4 were operating without authorization. |
| 2 | Egypt | The Supreme Council of Universities (SCU) and the National Quality Assurance Accreditation and Agency (NQAAA) | 2004 | Semi | 12 | 14 | SCU has mandate over the establishment of national and foreign institutions. NQAAA, established in 2004 has mandate for QA and accreditation. |
| 3 | Ethiopia | Quality Relevance and Assurance Agency (QRAA) | 2003 | No | 7 | 30 | Institutional accreditation. As of October 2005, Ethiopia had 30 private tertiary institutions. |
| 4 | Ghana | National Accreditation Board (NAB) | 1993 | Semi | 7 | 14 | Accredits public & private institutions and programs. Determines the equivalence of diplomas. |
| 5 | Kenya | Commission for Higher Education (CHE) | 1985 | Semi | 6 | 17 | Accreditation of institutions and programs. Standardization, recognition of degrees. |
| 6 | Liberia | National Commission on Higher Education (NCHE) | 2000 | Semi | 3 | 1 | Has mandate for accreditation of HEIs, setting standards for admission and credit transfer, and disbursement of government subsidies to accredited institutions. |

(*Continued*)

Table A.1. Countries with Legally Established National QA Agencies (*Continued*)

| | Country | QA Authority | Year Created | Level of Autonomy* | Public HEIs | Private HEIs | Mandate of QA Agency |
|---|---|---|---|---|---|---|---|
| 7 | Mauritius | Tertiary Education Commission (TEC) | 1997 | Semi | 4 | 35 | Public and private institutional audits and program accreditation. As of August 2006, there were 35 private tertiary institutions and 50 overseas institutions & bodies delivering tertiary education. |
| 8 | Mozambique | Ministry of Higher Education, Science & Technology | 2003 | Semi | 3 | 2 | Sets criteria of establishing new institutions. Is currently defining accreditation. |
| 9 | Namibia | National Council for Higher Education (NCHE) | 2004 | No | 2 | 1 | Evaluates registration of private institutions & accreditation of courses. Also to promote accountability of HEIs. |
| 10 | Nigeria | The National Universities Commission (NUC) | 1990 | Semi | 41 | 8 | Examines curricula, advises the government on HE development, establishes academic standards and their enforcement, responsible for accreditation and ranking of universities. |
| 11 | South Africa | HEQC under Council on Higher Education (CHE) | 2001 | Semi | 25 | 1 | Institutional audits and program accreditation. |
| 12 | Sudan | Evaluation and Accreditation Corporation (EVAC) | 2003 | No | 33 | 15 | Oversees university academic reviews. |
| 13 | Tanzania | The Higher Education Accreditation Council (HEAC) | 1995 | Semi | 11 | 19 | Has mandate for licensing of new HEIs, institutional & program accreditation as well as university academic audits/reviews. |

| | | | | | | | |
|---|---|---|---|---|---|---|---|
| 14 | Tunisia | Commité national d'Evaluation | 1995 | Semi | 18 | 8 | |
| 15 | Uganda | National Commission for Higher Education (NCHE) | 2005 | Semi | 4 | 12 | Institutional audit & accreditation; university academic review. |
| 16 | Zimbabwe | National Council for Higher Education (NCHE) | 2006 | No | 8 | 5 | Institutional visitations and inspections; advises government, ensures the maintenance of appropriate standards. NCHE was established in 2006. |

* A semi-autonomous agency has its own establishing law, independent board and budget allocation. Makes final decision on accreditation or audit.

**Table A.2. Countries Without National QA Agencies**

| | Country | QA Authority | Public HEIs | Private HEIs | Comments |
|---|---|---|---|---|---|
| 1 | Algeria | Ministry | 25 | N/A | The Ministry of Higher Education & Scientific Research has mandate over public institutions. Private higher education is insignificant. |
| 2 | Angola | Ministry | 2 | 5 | No evidence of QA processes. |
| 3 | Benin | Ministry | 1 | 27 | The Ministry for Higher Education licenses establishment of private institutions. |
| 4 | Botswana | Ministry | 1 | 0 | No evidence of QA processes. |
| 5 | Burkina Faso | Ministry | 2 | 1 | No evidence of QA processes. |
| 6 | Burundi | Government responsible for central admin & coordination | 6 | | No evidence of QA processes. |
| 7 | Cape Verde | Ministry | 1 | 0 | No evidence of QA processes. |
| 8 | Central Africa Republic | Ministry | 1 | N/A | Only one private institution. No info if QA is required. |
| 9 | Chad | Ministry | 1 | N/A | The only university is characterized by high failure rate—INHEA. |
| 10 | Comoros | N/A | 0 | 0 | No universities. |
| 11 | Congo-Brazzaville | Ministry | 1 | 1 | Limited system for recognition of private institutions established in 1990. |
| 12 | Congo DRC | Ministry | 46 | 12 | Ministry of Education licenses establishment of new HEIs. Over 250 private HEIs authorized by April 2006. |
| 13 | Cote D'Ivoire | Ministry | 3 | 3 | Ministry licenses establishment of new local and foreign HEIs. 37 authorized by 2000. |
| 14 | Djibouti | Ministry | 1 | 0 | No information. |
| 15 | Eritrea | Ministry | 1 | 0 | Government is responsible for QA; no private universities. |
| 16 | Gabon | Ministry | 3 | 2 | No evidence of any QA activities. |
| 17 | Gambia, The | Ministry | 1 | 0 | No information. |
| 18 | Guinea | Ministry | 3 | 3 | Government liberalization policy to regulate establishment of private institutions. |

*(Continued)*

**Table A.2. Countries Without National QA Agencies (*Continued*)**

| | Country | QA Authority | Public HEIs | Private HEIs | Comments |
|---|---|---|---|---|---|
| 19 | Guinea-Bissau | Ministry | 0 | 0 | No public nor private universities. |
| 20 | Lesotho | Ministry | 1 | 0 | University academic review conducted. |
| 21 | Libya | Ministry | 16 | 5 (as of 2000) | Mandate over national institutions to develop educational content. |
| 22 | Madagascar | Ministry | 6 | 16 (as of 2003) | University academic review. Establishment of a QA agency underway. The 16 private HEIs are part of the Association of Private Establishments in Higher Education operating under a special agreement with the Ministry of Education. |
| 23 | Malawi | Ministry | 4 | 1 | No evidence of HE quality assurance processes at the national level. |
| 24 | Mali | Ministry | 1 | 0 | Establishment of first private university under way. No information as to whether accreditation is required. |
| 25 | Mauritania | Ministry | 3 | N/A | No information in the public domain on how quality assurance is implemented. |
| 26 | Morocco | Ministry | 14 | 203 (2003/ 4 estimate) | The Ministry of Higher Education, Staff Training and Scientific Research ensures quality education. Of the 203 private HEIs, 162 are business schools. |
| 27 | Niger | Ministry | 1 | 1 | No information on whether accreditation is required. |
| 28 | Rwanda | Ministry | 3 | 4 | QA is a current challenge facing the government. |
| 29 | Sao Tome & Principe | Ministry | 0 | 1 | First higher education institution established in 1994. |
| 30 | Senegal | Ministry | 4 | NA | Limited recognition of private institutions is being developed. |
| 31 | Seychelles | Ministry | 0 | 0 | No higher education institutions. |
| 32 | Sierra Leone | Ministry | 2 | N/A | Massive destruction of education infrastructure and displacement of teachers. |
| 33 | Somalia | Ministry | 0 | 8 | No government regulation but the Ministry of Education (unrecognized) has set minimum standards. |

(*Continued*)

**Table A.2. Countries Without National QA Agencies (*Continued*)**

| | Country | QA Authority | Public HEIs | Private HEIs | Comments |
|---|---|---|---|---|---|
| 34 | Swaziland | Ministry | 1 | N/A | No private universities. The only public university is assumed to be accredited. |
| 35 | Togo | Ministry | 3 | N/A | Only 1 public university; no private universities. |
| 36 | Zambia | Ministry. | 2 | 0 | Monitoring of standards of education. The 2 public universities are assumed accredited by Act of Parliament. No private universities. The Examination Council of Zambia (ECZ) has responsibility for examinations. |

# References

## Background Case Studies

Jibril, Munzali, 2006. "Quality Assurance and Accreditation in Higher Education in Nigeria."

Mihyo, Paschal. 2006. "Quality Assurance and Accreditation in Higher Education in Tanzania."

Mohamedbhai, Goolam. 2006. "Quality Assurance in Mauritius Higher Education."

Ncayiyana, Daniel, J. 2006. "Higher Education Quality Assurance and Accreditation in South Africa."

Saffu, Y. 2006. "Quality Assurance and Accreditation in Higher Education in Ghana."

Titanji, V. 2006. "Quality Assurance and Accreditation in Higher Education in Cameroon."

## Other References

Adu, Kingsley and François Orivel, 2006. *Tertiary Education Funding Strategy in Ghana.* Report to the National Council of Tertiary Education. Accra, Ghana.

Bloom, David, David Canning, and Kevin Chan. 2006. "Higher Education and Economic Development in Africa." Africa Region Human Development Working Paper Series No. 102. Washington, D.C.: The World Bank.

Brossard, M., and B. Foko. 2006. "Couts et financement de l'enseignement superieur dans les pays d'Afrique francophone." Pole de Dakar (UNESCO BREDA). Paper presented at the Francophone Higher Education Conference, Ouagadougou, June.

Commission for Higher Education (CHE). 2006. "A Handbook on Processes, Standards and Guidelines for Quality Assurance." January Draft. Kenya.

Council for Higher Education Accreditation (CHEA). 2002. "Accreditation and Assuring Quality in Distance Learning." CHEA Monograph Series, Number 1. http://www.chea.org/pdf/mono_1_accred_distance_02.pdf?pubID=246

De Pietro-Jurand, Robin, and Maria Jose Lemaitre. 2002. "Quality Assurance in Colombia." The World Bank, Washington, D.C. Processed.

Docquier, Frédéric, and Abdeslam Marfouk. 2005. "International Migration by Educational Attainment 1990-2000." World Bank Policy Research Working Paper No. 3382, The World Bank, Washington, D.C.

El-Khawas, E., R. DePietro-Jurand, and L. Holm-Nielsen. 1998. "Quality Assurance in Higher Education: Recent Progress; Challenges Ahead." Prepared for UNESCO World Conference on Higher Education, Paris, France, October 5–9.

Hall, Martin. 2005. "Quality Assurance at UCT." Version 5, undated. www.ched.uct.ac.za/qaprojects.htm (accessed November 20, 2005).

Hanushek, E.A., and L. Wossmann. 2007. "The Role of Education Quality in Economic Growth." World Bank Policy Research Working Paper No. 4122, The World Bank, Washington, D.C.

Hayward, Fred M. 2000. "Multi-lateral Agreements That Address International Quality Assurance," CHEA. www.chea.org/international/multi-lateral.html.
Ishumi, A., and M. Nkunya. 2003. "Improvements in the Quality of Education: The University of Dar es Salaam Experience with an Academic Audit." A case study paper prepared for the Regional Training Conference on Improving Tertiary Education in Sub-Saharan Africa: Things That Work, September.
Kiamba, Crispus. 2003. "The Experience of the Privately Sponsored Studentship and Other Income Generating Activities at the University of Nairobi." A case study prepared for the Regional Training Conference "Improving Tertiary Education in Sub-Saharan Africa: Things that Work!", Accra, Ghana, September 23–25.
Liu, N.C., and Y. Cheng. 2005. "Academic Ranking of World Universities—Methodologies and Problems." *Higher Education in Europe* 30(2).
Materu, P. 2006. "Talking Notes." Conference on Knowledge for Africa's Development, Johannesburg, South Africa, May.
National Universities Commission (NUC). 2002. *Ranking of Universities According to Performance of their Academic Programs in 1991 and 2000.*
———. 2006. *NUC Monday Memo* 5(3).
Newsweek International. 2006. "The Complete List: The Top 100 Global Universities." August 13.
Okebukola, P. 2006. "Quality Assurance in Higher Education: The Nigerian Experience." Paper presented at the Quality Assurance in Tertiary Education Conference, Sevres, France, June 18–20.
Ramcharan, R. 2004. "Higher Education or Basic Education: The Composition of Human Capital and Economic Development." *IMF Staff Papers* 51(2). Washington, D.C.: International Monetary Fund.
SAUVCA. 2002. *Quality Assurance in South African Universities.* Views from SAUVCA's National Quality Assurance Forum.
Shabani, J. 2006. *Higher Education in French Speaking Sub-Saharan Africa.* UNESCO Harare Cluster Office, Zimbabwe.
UNESCO. 2006. *Guidelines for Quality Provision in Cross-border Higher Education.* Paris.
University of The Gambia. 2005. "The UTG Strategic Plan." Processed.
World Bank. 1994. *Higher Education: Lessons of Experience.* Washington, D.C.
———. 2002. *Constructing Knowledge Societies: New Challenges for Tertiary Education.* Washington, D.C.
———. 2004a. "Higher Education Development for Ethiopia: Pursuing the Vision." Washington, D.C.
———. 2004b. "Mid-Term Review of the Mozambique Higher Education Project." Processed.
———. 2004c. "Project Appraisal Document—Federal Democratic Republic of Ethiopia Post-Secondary Project."
———. 2005. "Meeting the Challenge of Africa's Development: A World Bank Group Action Plan." Processed.
———. 2006. "Final Report: Francophone Higher Education Conference." June. http://www.worldbank.org/education/ouagadougou

# Eco-Audit

## Environmental Benefits Statement

The World Bank is committed to preserving Endangered Forests and natural resources. We print World Bank Working Papers and Country Studies on 100 percent postconsumer recycled paper, processed chlorine free. The World Bank has formally agreed to follow the recommended standards for paper usage set by Green Press Initiative—a nonprofit program supporting publishers in using fiber that is not sourced from Endangered Forests. For more information, visit www.greenpressinitiative.org.

In 2006, the printing of these books on recycled paper saved the following:

| Trees* | Solid Waste | Water | Net Greenhouse Gases | Total Energy |
|---|---|---|---|---|
| 203 | 9,544 | 73,944 | 17,498 | 141 mil. |
| *40' in height and 6–8" in diameter | Pounds | Gallons | Pounds $CO_2$ Equivalent | BTUs |